ALSO BY
EMILY BELLE FREEMAN

The Christ-Centered Home: Inviting Jesus In
Celebrating a Christ-Centered Christmas
Celebrating a Christ-Centered Easter

WITH DAVID BUTLER

The Peter Potential
Maybe Today

GETTING TO THE PLACE
WHERE YOU CAN TRUST GOD
WITH ANYTHING

Even This

EMILY BELLE FREEMAN

ENSIGN
PEAK

Interior images: Zebra Finch/shutterstock.com

Visit us at ShadowMountain.com

Library of Congress Cataloging-in-Publication Data

(CIP data on file)
ISBN 978-1-62972-338-9

Printed in the United States of America
Lake Book Manufacturing, Inc., Melrose Park, IL

10 9 8 7 6 5 4 3 2 1

*For the one who wondered
if she could ever trust God again.*

Contents

CONTENTS

SECTION THREE: UNDERSTANDING WHY SOMETIMES HE DOESN'T

Until the Story Is Your Own

The dull brick walkway marks a solid contrast to the lush green lawn growing outside the cement building standing behind us. The afternoon sun blazes, the air swelters, and my heart pounds out the unsteady rhythm that follows a rush of uncertainty. We gather in silence outside the gray walls that hold the pain, the reality still raw.

Standing in the light, we think we have left the darkness inside with the mounds of shaved hair, the leather shoes piled high, and the black-and-white footage that doesn't lie. We stand in the light, but we can't shake the shadows. They cling to us, settling deep into our memories, never to be forgotten, leaving darkness like a footprint on the soul.

It's not long before the silence between us is shattered, and now I stare at my younger sister, silently pleading with her to take back the words that had just come spilling out of her mouth: "I don't think I believe in God anymore."

I know exactly what she is thinking. *If God is real, how could He have let this happen? Why? Why, God?*

It was the first time in my short life I had ever heard the fear spoken aloud.

Is God good?

Can He be trusted?

Because where was God when six million of His people were killed?

Where was His goodness?

I don't remember how we moved past that somber afternoon—but we did. Perhaps the Holocaust Museum was absorbed into the Natural Museum of American History and the National Gallery of Art, and the embers somehow settled like so many ashes between the historical documents and colorful paintings. With time, what burned heavy and hot was blown carelessly away with the winds of ordinary life. The memories faded and so did the questioning, and we returned home, and went to church, and believed in God.

Perhaps you have experienced it. You know how it is— how we see the injustice, the unfairness, the death, the hatred, the pain, the anguish. And while it is there, in front of us, we feel the bitterness and sorrow. But there is something about the walking away that numbs us, and somehow we forget the fear and the doubt.

Until the story is our own.

Until the story is *your* own, and the pain isn't housed within cold museum walls, but burns a hot ache into the flesh of your heart and you feel as if life will never be ordinary again.

Believing He Can

Discovering God's Goodness

If you had told me when my children were small that they would all pick the same year to get married, I would have told you that you were crazy. Even if you had told me just one year ago that four of the five of them would find their soul mates at the same time and start planning back-to-back weddings, I still would have questioned your sanity.

People ask me all the time, "How did you do it?!" And it is a good question. Even now as I sit here and look at the photographs, I wonder, *how did we do it?* Four weddings in seven months. I, too, find it hard to believe. "The answer is simple," I tell everyone who asks. "The main floor of our home turned into Wedding Central." Each corner was decorated according to the wedding that was stationed there. For the better part of a year people walked into our home at their own risk.

I look around the room that is completely clean now, but I remember what it used to look like. The white banner letters hung from silk ribbon with navy tassels. The apothecary jars with pearls glued around the top, waiting to hold the dozens and dozens of soft pink peonies. The piles of ivory lace doilies and old-fashioned crocheted handkerchiefs purchased from the antique store. Old pallets, white picture frames, tiny glass jars hung from jute, aspen wood centerpieces, handmade quilts, dangling glass garlands, and the photographs. There were photographs everywhere. Engagement photos, bridal photos, first-look photos. Every moment captured so it would forever be remembered.

The upstairs room on the left became the brides' room. Only the girls were allowed entrance. There we hung the gowns, four gowns, each one so different from the others. The cream satin gown with sparkled pearl sequins from the scalloped neck to the very end of the train. Another made completely from ivory lace, with a pair of coral shoes that barely peeked out from under the hem. The third, a classic vintage design made from white satin and fine English lace strips, with a white, four-inch sash around the waist. The last, sewn from beautiful lace, with huge taffeta roses making up the entire skirt. Oh, the gowns, each almost as elegant as the bride who chose it.

Now the weddings are over, and I come into this room often to look at these photographs, to count blessings, and to remind myself what I have recently come to believe—that wedding days are filled with magic, miracles, and yes, even happy endings.

But that hasn't always been the case.

It is four days before the happiest day of my life. The satin and lace hang pressed and ready, the hand-sewn veil is finished and waiting, the white roses and gardenias have been ordered, and we sit behind closed doors in sterile quarters for the news. Greg is sick. We consider allergies, strep throat, or a winter cold, but the doctor fears something worse. We see it in his eyes, in the way he touches the same spot on Greg's throat two times, three times, and then just one more time before he leaves the room.

When the doctor returns he asks if we can postpone the wedding. The happiest day of my life. The one I've been dreaming of since I was twelve. The celebration I lay awake nights planning—the right colors, the right flowers, the right song. The invitations are sent; flights have been booked. We can't postpone the wedding. We won't. "How long is the honeymoon?" he asks. He is serious. I am twenty, and we are invincible, and our wedding is in four days. *Four days.* I try to think seriously, but the butterflies and the anticipation and the nearness of the celebration cloud out what he is saying. There is a possibility that Greg has thyroid cancer. An appointment with an oncologist is made for when we return from the honeymoon. We put the thought of it in the back of our minds as soon as we leave the urgent care clinic and drive back to the house to finalize the wedding plans and continue on with the celebration.

I would tell you about the wedding, but my memories of that short week are shrouded by what happened when it was over. The biopsy, the surgery, the three months of recovery—those are the memories that fill my mind when I think about the beginning of our marriage. What were supposed to be our first blissful days actually turned into hours spent waiting on pins and needles for results. The nights were filled with pain. The days with worry. Three months of recovery meant three months without work. We had no money; I remember how we barely got by on nothing. Maybe some people picture their wedding day in vivid detail. The memory I remember most from those first days actually took place at two in the morning in a dark hospital room.

It was after the surgery to remove the tumor, after Greg's mother and father left to go home. After the last doctor walked out and the pain meds were administered. After making the decision to spend the night at the hospital because I didn't want to go home alone. That's when it all finally hit. It was years ago, before there were comfortable sofas in hospital rooms, and I remember it as if it were yesterday.

I pull the orange plastic chair over to the hospital bed and reach under the stiff white sheet to find the warmth of Greg's hand. In that moment, I hold on to all that is familiar; I hold desperately to the dreams I used to know. The monitor beats a steady rhythm as I lay my head down on the rough green blanket. I wonder if those dreams will have to change now. Change is never easy, but this change, this unexpected change to my happily ever after, echoes through the corners of my heart. Is twenty years enough to prepare someone for this much uncertainty? Because I don't feel prepared for this. The loneliness frightens me. I am alone in this. It's dark, and Greg's parents have driven home, and my parents live hundreds of miles away, and Greg is here, but he is sedated. I am alone.

I see soft light flooding in under the door and I focus

there, on the truth that all is not dark. I try to remember that. But there, in that dark moment, the tears start to fall. There is no one to talk to, cry to, lean on, and so I pray. I talk to God and I tell Him I am frightened, I am too young for this, I am alone in this. I am alone. There, leaning over the hospital bed, clutching the hand of my new husband, I weep. And in the silent stillness of it all, an intense feeling of love fills the room and a whisper of words settles into my soul. It is a thread of scriptures I have read a hundred times, pieced together, meant to mend what is broken in my heart. I want to write the words down. I reach for the paperback book sitting on the small table and try to find a pen. I hold on to the words as I search—I don't want to forget them, the promise of them, so I whisper them out loud as I look. Finally, I find a pen, turn to the blank pages at the back of the newsprint book, and begin to write.

Early morning, January 1990

> *I can't describe this moment. It's almost as if I could reach out and touch the feeling in this room. For the first time I realize I've lived my whole life watching but never really seeing. Never knowing I was not alone. Maybe I never took the time to understand. Sometimes it has to hurt to make you strong, to make you realize how much you need God. I don't want to forget this. These words. His words. **Draw near unto me and I will draw near unto you. My peace I give to you. Be still, and know that I am God.***

The handwriting is scribbled, scattered across the pages, but the words won't be forgotten, and that is all that matters. For the first time I realize that I can turn to God with the real things, that I can *trust* Him with the hard things, with anything, *even this*. It is the first time I realize that God, who is infinite, can also be personal. For some reason, knowing that the Creator of the entire universe could be aware of a young, frightened girl in a dark hospital room strengthens my heart. I carry those whispered words as the healing days turn into weeks and then into months, until finally it is over and Greg is well and life begins to move forward again.

You wonder why that memory is more vivid than my wedding day. Perhaps it is because that experience, there in that dark hospital room, was the first time I had ever met God in an intimate space. It was the first time I had let myself be vulnerable with Him. The rawness led me to experience His realness. In that moment I felt His goodness.

> It was the first time I had let myself be **vulnerable** with Him. The rawness led me to experience His **realness**.

Maybe there was a first time for you. Maybe you hold on to the memory of it just like I do. You'd think after an experience like that, my heart would have been won for life.

But it isn't so.

One experience with God's goodness doesn't tie you to Him forever.

Tethered

She sits next to the red brick wall under the hot sun in the middle of the old city market. I watch her hands work. She has memorized this process, this making of baskets. Her eyes linger on the people walking through the streets. She rarely looks down; her fingers know instinctively what to do. The basket begins with one knot. A single knot. Everything leads out from there. Her fingers work the yellow grass over and through, over and through, tethering each piece against the last. There are no gaps, no open spaces—the basket is meant for holding in. I watch, fascinated by the process, drawn to the smell of sweet grass, and I am reminded of another basket, handcrafted just as this one is. Meant for God's purpose, for His goodness, even though it was woven in heartache.

I have heard the story a thousand times; sometimes it feels as if I am becoming expert in the learning of it. It is a story about tethering, about tracing God's goodness, about choosing whether or not to give a heart to God. You have heard it told. How the baby's mother places him, tiny and helpless, into the handwoven sweet grass basket, how his sister stands at the brink to watch him float down the river alone, how the daughter of Pharaoh comes down at just the right time and lifts him out. The daughter who was unknowingly sent to bring about God's goodness—God was aware of even this.

I read later, when the baby has grown, about the angel appearing in a flame of burning fire out of the bush there in the wilderness. I learn that Moses did not pass by unknowingly—he turned aside to see, he took off his shoes. Moses made himself vulnerable there in the wilderness, and because of that, he experienced God's realness. In doing so, he learned that the God who created the whole universe could be intimately aware of a shepherd standing next to a bush. But even more important, he learned that God could see the affliction of His people, He could hear their cry, He knew their sorrows, and He would come down to deliver them (see Exodus 3:7–8).

But, one experience with God's goodness doesn't tie you to Him forever.

I read that Moses questioned God about the purpose He had in store for him, and when I feel Moses' worry, his inadequacy, his uncertainty, for a minute I walk in his shoes. I have been there, where Moses is. I have questioned God. But there is hope in God's answer to Moses: "I will be with you. . . . You will not go empty" (Exodus 3:12, 21). Yes, there is hope, but it doesn't completely dispel the doubt.

"They will not believe me," Moses whispers. He has spoken to the Lord, been rescued by the Lord; he has been given promises by the Lord, and *still* there is doubt. I know that doubt. I, too, would have run from the serpent. Just like Moses, I would have suffered the leprosy. And even when God sends the rod and the healing, still, like Moses, I wonder. "Go," God says, "and I will be with you" (see Exodus 3). He says it to Moses, and to the children of Israel, and to me and you, and still, we falter.

Because one experience with God's goodness doesn't tie us to Him forever.

We see the miracles and believe, we walk into the wilderness believing, and then, when the path ahead becomes hard and the Red Sea lies before us, we question our belief. No, we don't question. We rebel against that belief. We think it would have been better for us to stay in Egypt. To stay in bondage. When we can't see the end in sight, we decide it is better for us to go back to what we knew. We can understand bondage. It isn't comfortable, but it is safe, and we know what to do there.

This vulnerable position, this intimacy with God, is uncomfortable. It stretches us beyond our own capacities. We question Him. We question ourselves. We question everything. Fear has a way of minimizing God's miracles, making it easy to walk away from belief. The only way to avoid this walking away is to trace His goodness throughout the journey. God understands this, so He sends another miracle, a reminder: "I will be

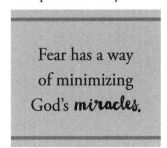

Fear has a way of minimizing God's *miracles.*

with you." We walk through what once had the potential to drown us on *dry* ground. The water doesn't just part. The mud, the sludge, the mess is taken care of too. The ground we walk on is dry. *He is aware of the little details.* Hope is restored, and we learn once again what it is to believe (see Exodus 14).

Until we are hungry, starving, until we might die from starvation, until the memory of the miracle pales against this current want—this desperate need—we hunger. The ache inside of us cries out for relief, and we aren't certain this God who can move water can satisfy a daily want. He is the God of big things, we assume, but does He care about this? *Even this?* So we murmur, and we consider going back to what was easier. Maybe it is easier to live without God, to remain in bondage. We understand bondage.

But in the morning God sends the manna. Bread from heaven. God's mercy sent down daily, gathered daily, gathered according to each person's need. *How much would I take?* I wonder. Of the Lord's goodness, how much do I take? The children of Israel gather it every morning, according to their need. Every morning. For forty years. The Lord is with them every morning, filling them, providing for them *every single morning,* but it isn't long before the mercies become mundane. "We loathe this bread," they say out loud (see Numbers 21). There is no gratitude. There is hatred. The water spills from a rock, a tabernacle is raised from the dust, they walk away from Caleb and Joshua's land of milk and honey. Why? Because of unbelief? Because they have forgotten His goodness? Because they have set aside gratitude?

Do I?

Because I think I have taken steps into the unknown with God, looked at the wilderness ahead, and thought about turning back. I have faced the unconquerable with no way around, no way across, no way through, and I have felt small, wondering if God has forgotten me. I know the wanting that presses down hard, the aching for relief, the certainty that there is no way out. The questioning if God is great enough for this. The questioning if God even cares about this. *I know what that is.*

And I wonder how many times I have taken what God could have made holy and instead made it into my own mischief. The gold, tried in the fire—do I corrupt it with my doubt? Because there, in the burning, what is meant for the tabernacle somehow becomes a calf (see Exodus 32:19–24).

I am guilty of pointing fingers. I scoff at Israel. I wonder, when they had seen so many miracles, when they had lived through so many personal experiences with God, how could they choose to walk away? How could they substitute a cold, unmoving, unfeeling object for a God who was willing to walk through the wilderness beside them? To walk through fire and water with them? To provide, and rescue, and deliver? When they could so easily trace His goodness through the everyday moments of their lives, how could they walk away?

Why is it that those experiences with God's goodness didn't tie them to Him forever?

The silence condemns me. It reminds me that I have considered walking away. When the hope of God becomes uncertain, when the waiting game takes its toll, when the answers don't come in *my* timing, in *my* way, when they don't meet *my* expectations. It's true; my heart has considered walking away. Yes, I have heard this story a thousand times; sometimes it feels as if I am becoming expert in the learning of it. Because the story is mine. I am Israel.

And I have considered giving up the risk of God for the convenience of the golden calf.

It is not hard for me to imagine Moses taking the calf, burning it in the fire, grinding it to powder, and making the children of Israel drink it (see Exodus 32:20). I take the cup, and I drink it down. I drink the mischief, every single bit of it, and I realize I am not filled. It cannot fill me. There is only One who can fill me.

Could I tether my heart to Him? Could I open my life to the prospect of making room for daily personal experiences with God? Could I learn to trace His goodness?

I hear the call of Moses to the children of Israel: "Who is on the Lord's side? let him come to me" (Exodus 32:26).

And I wonder if I will come.

The Other Calf

Outside the upstairs window I see the leaves of the shade tree moving with the afternoon wind, and I feel guilt. The branches hang low, sighing with the added weight. Soft red and golden orange, the harvest fruit waits, ready. My tongue anticipates the sweetness, and yet I do not go down. It's been three days now, the tree waiting, ready, and I don't go out the back door and through the picket fence to the waiting goodness. I still have not gone. Truth be told, I am afraid of the bees that hover round, I don't want to face the sweltering heat, and I don't know where I am going to put all of the fully ripened fruit. So the branches hang low, and they wait. If I don't go soon the birds will come, the fruit will spoil, it will fall to the ground—a perfect harvest wasted. The guilt hovers with the weight of goodness ignored, and I am burdened by it. And even still, I do not go down.

I am reminded of the two sons of a good father. You will know this story. You will have heard it time and time again, and maybe there will be a part of you that wants to skip through this. Don't. Because before the story begins, a question must be posed. In order to understand this story fully, I ask myself the question from which there is no hiding: which of the sons am I?

The younger son lived in discontent. There is no knowing the root of it; we only know the asking for more than just a gift, the asking for everything, his whole portion, all of his father's living. And we know that, in not so many days, it was gone. Wasted with riotous living. Not only did this son waste his inheritance, he wasted his substance, he sold his whole soul. When it was all spent, when *he* was all spent, and it was gone, all of it, *gone,* a famine came into the land. Before, there had been discontent, but now the younger son really knew what it was to want. That want led him to let go of his status and his pride and eventually his belief, and in leaving it he was left alone with no one to care for him. Until, finally, he came to himself. Because underneath the discontent and the wasted, riotous living, underneath the pride and the false beliefs, there was still the father's youngest son.

Memories of goodness run deep, and so it was in this case. In the son's hunger and his want, he remembered his father and the bread he fed to his servants—enough, and some to spare. What drew the son home was the thought of his father, *of his father's goodness,* and so he arose and went.

The verses talk about the boy rising early in the morning to go to his father and how his father saw him coming when he was still a great way off, and I pause and realize the father had been watching. All of this time, the father had been watching. Waiting. For the son he knew would come. The father did not want to miss the coming home. And when he saw his son, the father's heart filled with compassion and he ran, and fell on his son's neck, and kissed him. *He met him where he was.* Before the apology could be given, before recompense could be made, the father held him. In that moment the boy began to understand. He did not have to be perfect to be welcome in his father's home. He did not have to be perfect to qualify for his father's love. He did not have to be perfect to earn his father's goodness.

But the beginning of understanding does not lead to a fullness, and so the son poured out his regret. "I have sinned, and I am no longer worthy to be called your son" (see Luke 15). The father did not answer. Instead he asked for the best robe and a ring for his son's hand and shoes for his feet. He clothed his son in his finest. Clothing not fit for a servant, but for a son. *His* son. He was still his father's son. He had been all along.

Here, in this part of the story, I read about another calf. Not a golden calf, but a fatted calf. A calf that had been prepared. I remember how this story is a parable and consider the meaning the parable must have held the first time it was told. I contemplate the people who first heard the story told by Jesus, I think about the setting and the context, and I realize these were people who could understand the layers of symbolism shrouded within a sacrifice, and I think how the good father had prepared all along for this fatted calf.

I read how the older son draws near, how he hears the music and the dancing. There is a celebration, and he is angry. He is mad about the fatted calf and the younger son returning home. His father killed the fatted calf, and now he will not go in. So the father comes out. *He meets his son where he is.* Instead of a rebuke, instead of a reprimand, the father listens. And in that moment, if he had chosen to, the boy would have understood. He did not have to be perfect to be welcome in his father's home. He did not have to be perfect to qualify for his father's love. He did not have to be perfect to earn his father's goodness.

> He did not have to be *perfect* to be welcome in his father's home. He did not have to be *perfect* to qualify for his father's love. He did not have to be *perfect* to earn his father's goodness.

But the beginning of understanding does not lead to a fullness, and so the older son pours out his anger. "For these years I have served you, I have not gone against you, and you never gave me anything like this. But as soon as this younger son came home, your son who lost everything in sin, you killed the fatted calf for him" (see Luke 15). Still there is no rebuke, no reprimand. Instead, the good father gives a gentle reminder. "You will always be with me, you have always been with me, and all that I have is yours. All of this goodness, even the fatted calf. It has been all along" (see Luke 15). In that moment, if he had chosen to, the boy would have seen a father who had always been there, who did not require any more than what the son could give. A father who was offering full access to everything he had, full access to the goodness, full access to the fatted calf.

The close of the chapter reminds us once again of the father's goodness, and then the verses end. But the story doesn't end. There is no answer, and we are left wondering. Will the elder brother go in? Will he enter the celebration and be glad? Will he partake of the fatted calf?

Would I?

The story ends, and it leaves me asking the question that hovers with the weight of goodness ignored, and I am burdened by it.

I read the story and I see myself there in the field, just like the two sons. I am the younger son, and I am in the field, and I want, because I have wasted and spent what could have been mine. I am the elder son, and I am in the field, and I have plenty, but I do not see it because of pride, because of ingratitude, because of what I believe I am owed for simply being in the field. The Father watches this. He watches, and He waits. I am in the field, and He watches for the moment my heart will soften, for me to take the first step toward Him, and He meets me there in that place, and He listens.

All along, there is the Father's goodness.

Just inside, the fatted calf has been prepared. It is there, in the middle of the celebration, waiting. With it comes the promise of sustenance, of nourishment, the savor of goodness. Will I go in, or will I pass it by—a perfect sacrifice wasted? What am I afraid of? What is it I don't want to face? What holds me back? I stand in the field and I can't help but ask myself, *which son am I?*

And I wonder, *will I partake of the fatted calf?*

To Believe

A cicada counts out a rhythm in the trees, and I feel the breeze stirring the beginnings of fall. We have gathered, like we do, the seven of us who have decided to devote one summer night every week to talk about scripture. I am old in their eyes, but still they invite me. The others are the age of my daughter, they are in high school, and I marvel at their desire to believe in God, to believe in His goodness. They each take a turn. Once a week they talk about the learning, they ask questions. The desire burns inside, and I see it there. It is tangible. One is tall and lanky. Black, trendy glasses frame his eyes, and he doesn't pull out his notes. He just starts talking. It is the summer before his senior year, and he has been studying what it means to yoke yourself with the Lord. It is his turn, and just like all of his turns before, all sixteen weeks of taking turns, he is talking about this yoke.

We sit on the Adirondack chairs in the backyard, the chairs that beg for a penetrating, soaking-in stain. As I look more intently at the wood that has been left uncared for far too long, he begins to talk. He doesn't share scripture.

He doesn't read a quote. He starts talking about the High Adventure camp last week, the one where they hiked thirteen miles. How he got to the top first, and, settling the weight of the journey down, sunk against a huge boulder and breathed to recover. "Those who are here could head back down the mountain and carry the packs of those who are struggling," the Scoutmaster hinted in invitation. But he was tired, this boy. Making it to the top first had taken everything out of him. Besides, there were others heading back to help. They would do it. And so he focused on breathing. On letting go of the weight of the journey. He didn't go.

It wasn't until the next day that the learning soaked in, soft like dew, but heavy with guilt. The yoke. The sharing of the burden. The study he had taken on for sixteen weeks this summer. He had done the learning of it, but what about the living of it? Sixteen weeks devoted to an intense study, and none of it had penetrated his soul. He hadn't gone back to help. He hadn't shared the burden.

It was on the third day, when they reached the bottom of the mountain, that the invitation was given again to those who had arrived first. Go back and help. Go back and lift the burden. The tall, lanky boy who had learned his lesson set down his pack and went. He hiked all the way back to the last straggler. He lifted the pack of the boy farthest behind and put it on his own back, and he didn't feel the weight. "And maybe that is how the yoke feels," he said. "Maybe sharing the burden really does make it lighter."

The group started talking. But we didn't talk about the yoke; we talked about the living. You can spend your whole life learning, studying—going to church, listening to the sermon, studying the Word, you might even take notes. But at what point does the learning part transition into the living part? When does what you believe turn into who you will become? When does it penetrate the heart? When does the soaking in take place?

We wrestle with this. The motions compared to the meaning. We decide it has to do with the desire with which you enter into the believing.

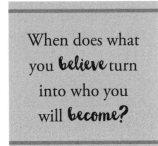

When does what you *believe* turn into who you will *become?*

I question the intent of my heart and consider the opportunities I have had to discover God's goodness this week. Did I take the time to look for it? To discover it within the ordinary details? Everything God had done for me, all of the goodness—had I noticed it? Could I even remember it? Where was my desire?

I lean into the reality of it and realize that I've settled down into the weight of the journey, and in doing so I might have set aside my desire to invest in this relationship with God. It becomes clear: desire is the first step to fully believing, to holding on to belief. And I wonder, *do I have the desire, an honest desire, to enter in?* Because tracing God's goodness will require me to yoke myself with Him. To invest myself. To become vulnerable. To believe.

I wonder, where are you in this journey? Where is the goodness, and where are the hard things, and where have you met God in the middle? What has it led you to believe?

I remember the scripture found in the tenth chapter of Hebrews: "We are not of those that draw back . . . but of them that believe" (Hebrews 10:39). I don't want to be known as someone who draws back. It is not like me to draw back. It leaves me wondering what I might be missing if I choose this drawing back.

So I decide to enter in.

The Crystal Vase

I enter in, but honestly it scares me a little bit. I have decided that maybe I hold God at arm's length. My belief is real—I am certain about that—but I think I might protect it like the cut glass vase I keep in the cupboard over the fridge. The crystal vase handed down from my grandma, the one that is precious to me, so precious that I don't want it to get broken. I keep it there, protected, in a place where it won't get dirty or damaged or disturbed. It is safe, but is that where I want it?

Because the other vase—the one that holds the marked-down roses I buy weekly from the grocery store, the deep purple iris from my yard, the flowers from the funeral, the wildflowers from the camping trip, the bouquet Greg sent on the day I really needed a lift—that vase sits out ready to be used. I use it so often that there isn't time to put it behind a closed door in a dark cupboard for the special occasion that only comes once a year. Why is it that I use daily the vase I don't even love the most?

Is that how it is with my relationship with God? Do I protect it from the hard things?

I take a good, hard look inside my soul, and when I go there I discover something I didn't know I would find. I love God, with my whole heart. I have for my whole life. I have gone through the motions of belief every day since I was born, *but have I really believed in His goodness?* Or have I sheltered the belief, protecting it from the hard things, the hard questions, the hard realities that can't be easily resolved, the ones that may never be resolved? Do I hold those things back from God? I realize that the knowing will require going back, all the way back to that sweltering day in D.C., to the first time I questioned if God was good. I will start there, and I will move along to the late night in the dark room of the University Hospital, and I will continue one by one to remember my encounters with God.

Some of them will be miraculous, and some will be painful, and maybe this heart needs to come to terms with that. Maybe, for this relationship to be real, my heart needs to come to understand that. Although I know it in my mind, maybe I need to reconcile that reality in my heart—choosing to follow God doesn't make life easy; it won't be easier. Because life is dirty, and my best plans are going to be frustrated, and sometimes my heart will feel the damage of that. And maybe the God I believe in is okay with digging through some dirt.

I consider it and I decide that for this relationship with God to be real, I can't look only for the times when everything worked out. I can't focus on only the miracles and the solutions that came packaged just the way I requested. I can't believe only in a God who gives exactly what I ask for. I will have to lean into the times when God let me down; I will have to remember the answers that never came. I won't ignore them. I will allow myself to consider all of it, and this time I won't keep score.

Instead, I will sort through the moments carefully to remember how God is aware of the conditions and particulars of my life. How not knowing increases the necessity for faith. How falling is what forces me to reach out for grace. How letting God be God might lead me to answers I didn't ask for, but ones that He knows I need. I want to look for the times in my life when He got right down in the dirt with me, and I want to trace the goodness that I discover there. His goodness. Even in the hard things. I want to discover Him in the hard things, because a belief in a God that only provides happy things isn't real. And I want it to be real, this relationship I have with God. There, in the dirt, it is there that I will discover how an infinite God can also be intimate. When I find Him there in the mess, when I gather the memory of His goodness, it leads to one truth that cannot be ignored: Someone who is willing to be there for you, walk through fire for you, dig through the dirt with you, fix the damage, enter the dark places, and the questioning places, and the aching places—the One who meets you in the most intimate places *must* love you.

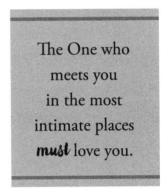

The One who meets you in the most intimate places *must* love you.

It is within the hard details that we discover the reality of that love, the depth of that love.

The truth of it settles into my soul. In the moments when I question His goodness, I must remember His love.

I look back and I can clearly trace those times when I have considered giving up the risk of God for the convenience of the golden calf, but I also see the moments when I have slowed down, entered in, and partaken of the fatted calf—when I have experienced His goodness. I trace those experiences and gather them so I will have a reminder. Those experiences define who God is in my life, and the looking back has led me to believe He is good. Even in the hard things.

I walk over to the cupboard that holds the crystal vase and open the knotted wood door. It is sitting safely there in the dark place where I keep it. As I open the door wider, light from the window behind me illuminates prisms off the cut glass. It is precious to me, this vase. I gently lift it out of the cupboard and carry it to the kitchen counter so I can fill it with this week's roses.

THE REFLECTING PLACE

Most evenings now I spend a moment in reflection. It has become a necessity, an end-of-day ritual, a soothing that comes before the slumber. I look back over the day, through the moments that someone else might glance over, that another might call a coincidence; it is in those raw places that I have learned to see His realness. So I pause, I reflect, and I trace His goodness. Perhaps you would like to try it, this reflecting, this tracing of God's goodness. Here is how it works.

I look for it there in the ordinary details—in the promptings I follow that lead to blessings, in the mercies that could be considered miracles, in the little things that hint at His tenderness.

Every single night I gather these details, I see the evidence of His fingerprint, and I remember.

He loves me.

It sounds simple, I know. And yet, it is powerful, this reflection time. It is tethering me to God. When I have finished remembering, after I have finished tracing the goodness, I express my gratitude to Him. I am learning that it is within the gratitude that I discover God's generosity, and within the generosity that I am reminded, once again, of His goodness.

Yes, He is good to me.

Trace the Goodness

The Place of Deepest Asking

It is fall, and I knock on the door of a good friend. Her mother answers, and without saying a word she points to a closed door down the hall. I walk down the hall and open the door and wait for my eyes to become accustomed to the dark. As I wait, I hear her muffled sobs from the corner. She is crying, her tears flowing down her cheeks, and slowly the picture begins to take shape. My friend is there in the corner of a small loveseat, sitting all closed up inside herself with a soft blanket pulled up to her quivering chin. I feel it, right when I walk in. It is tangible, the hopelessness—it blankets the room like fog. He has left her. He has taken away her hopes, he has lied, and he has taken away her pride. I don't ask for the details. I don't ask what happened, how it happened, when it happened. I ask the same question that she is asking, that she has asked since the moment he walked out. I know exactly what she is thinking. *If God is real, how could He have let this happen? Why? Why, God?*

Again, the fear of it is spoken out loud.

Is God good?

Can He be trusted?

It has been years since the museum, and yet the questions are the same. But what isn't the same is what I have come to know. There are times in our lives when answers cannot be found. The places where there are no answers become the catalysts for belief. I am certain of this: the place of deepest asking is where the believing begins.

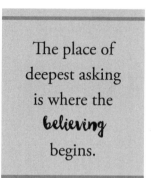

The place of deepest asking is where the *believing* begins.

I vow to enter into this asking place, this believing place, and I am ready for what comes next. It won't be easy, this journey. Believing is a dangerous way to live.

The only safety comes from tracing God's goodness through the good things and the hard things and an unfailing belief that through it all, through even this, He loves us. The outcome may be uncertain, but the reality of His love is not.

It is within that love that I come to believe. Yes, God is good.

But can He be trusted?

Trusting He Will

Falling

I listen to the simple explanation the lithe teenage girl gives to her younger sister. It is the first time the younger one has played this game. She is in kindergarten. Old enough now to begin to understand some things. Old enough to understand trust. The older sister explains how she will stand with arms outstretched to catch the younger girl. She will not move from that spot; she will be there. The younger sister listens with wide eyes, nodding her head, blonde hair bobbing off her shoulders. Finally she is ready to try. The older sister stands, arms out, ready. The younger faces away from her and closes her eyes. She is going to try this. It frightens her a little; I see it on her face. They count to three together and then the younger one starts falling backward. For a second I think she will do it, but then I watch her open her eyes wide, fling out her arms, take a step back, and turn her head toward her sister. "You didn't do it!" The older sister is laughing; her eyes twinkle with mirth. "You didn't trust me! I was right here and you didn't trust me."

"Let me do it!" The middle brother steps in now. He is

in second grade. Invincible. He's played this game before. He knows the older sister will not move. She will not fail. She will be there. She stands ready, and he turns to face away from her. They count to three together and then, straight as a board, he falls into her arms. She is fun. She does not catch him right at the beginning. She waits until the last minute. She is good at this game. And he is good also. He doesn't flinch in the waiting. He leans back and he knows. She will not let him fall.

The younger sister is ready to try again. She steps back into place. The older sister waits, ready. They begin counting again. "One, two, three!" The younger sister falls. She is straight as a board, just like her brother, eyes closed. I watch the older sister and I smile again. She doesn't wait for the last minute this time. Her arms are there right at the beginning. At the first second. She makes sure her sister knows she will not let her fall.

I am reminded of a favorite scripture: "Now unto Him that is able to keep you from falling . . . to the only wise God . . . be glory and majesty, dominion and power, both now and ever" (Jude 1:24–25). I see the truth of this verse defined in a child's game. I marvel that one can begin learning to trust at such a young age. I love that I see God's character there in the oldest sister.

This game, the trust fall, is a rite of passage. I have played it a hundred times, but I have watched it played even more times than I can count. My daughter Grace and I find a version of it on YouTube. We watch it over and over, because watching it once is not enough. We laugh straight from our bellies every time we see it. We begin laughing before it even begins, because we know what will happen, and because of the knowing the giggling can't be restrained.

It is a father teaching his two young girls about the trust fall. The older one knows what to do. She stands ready, knees bent, arms out. She bounces in place; she is serious about this, about doing this right. The younger sister asks to hear the instructions one more time, how she will face away from her sister, close her eyes, and fall. The dad begins to count, the older sister bends her knees, ready, and the younger sister begins to fall . . . *forward*. Yes, she falls forward. The dad forgot to explain which way to fall. Eyes closed, straight as a board, she falls. Right onto the floor. It is funny. Funny enough to watch again, and again, and just one more time.

Every time I see it, I laugh. But when I really think about it, I can't help but consider the reality of it. The reality of trust in a real world. Because what if I do fall? What happens when I fall? How do I learn to trust again? I wonder, did the sister in the video try again after that first attempt? We don't know. The video does not show it. I wonder if she did. I wonder if I would have. I have to think this through. Because now this is about more than just a game; it is about real life. I have learned to trace the goodness, to watch for God's love. I have felt it. But tracing the goodness doesn't mean that my life will only hold good things. I know the reality of it. Bad things happen to good people. I am going to fall. And when I do, will my heart still be capable of trust?

What if He lets me fall?

Alone in This

He is three years old. The two of us walk out of the hospital, out of the place of celebration. Today it is the place where new life, a newborn son, my nephew, has entered the world to find peace nestled in his mother's arms. As we walk outside, Josh complains about how the light hurts his eyes, it hurts his head. He whimpers and reaches his arms up, "Hold to you, Mommy," he says the way he always does, and I lift him into my arms the way I always do.

Josh and I get to the car and what was a whimper has turned into full tears, and as I buckle him in he begs me to cover his head with a cream and crimson blanket, the fringe around the edges sitting softly there on his lap. I tell myself he is tired; I tell myself he is cranky from waiting in the lobby for too many hours with his dad while I celebrated the beginning of new life upstairs. But as we pull onto the freeway he begins to throw up. I try to talk to him, try to help him, but he doesn't respond. I am in the middle of the freeway, and I don't know what to do, and through the closed eyes and the throwing up he just whimpers; he won't stop whimpering.

Until there is silence, and I drive to the only place I can think of for an emergency like this, and for some reason it isn't the hospital I just left. I drive to the office of my pediatrician, and I stand on the sidewalk, and I hold him unconscious in my arms, and I pound hard on the glass door because it is lunchtime and they have locked the door.

The details aren't important now. How they finally let us in and put us in a room. How I stripped him down to his navy blue and green plaid boxers and put all of his soaked-through belongings into a trash bag. How the soft pink sweater I was wearing reeked of the reality of whatever was going on. *What was going on?* How, in that wild moment, his doctor walked in from lunch and saw us sitting in the tiny room on the blue chair. Josh, fully unclothed and curled up into the pain and me trying to hold all of the pain and the unanswered questions and the fear—oh, the fear. How the doctor took one look at us and said, "It is diabetes. He has diabetes." And how a room was reserved for us at the children's hospital where we would go for five days and learn how to manage a disease we didn't want to have.

Five days later we leave the hospital and Josh thinks he is better. We walk out into the bitter November air and he clutches his teddy bear with his right fist and my hand with his left. He is happy, and I buckle him in his seat, and I sigh—we are going home. It is lunchtime when we get there. I unbuckle him from the seat and begin to unload everything from the car. He is not happy when he sees it—the needles, the meters, and the lancets that have become our reality, our way of life. He doesn't want that life. They let us go home from the hospital, and he is better now, and he doesn't need those things.

Josh is starving, and I lift him up on the counter to prick his little finger so it will bleed and tell him how the food he wants to eat will affect his tiny body. He starts crying the moment I pull out the black kit we brought home from the hospital. He squeezes his little hand into a fist and cries hot, angry tears. "I hate this." His mad voice is new; it came home with us from the hospital with all of the baggage we didn't want. "I hate you," he says, hot tears streaming down red cheeks. "You don't do this to anyone else in our family. You only do this to me. Why did you ever think I wanted to do this?"

I hold his hand tight, pulling his little fingers open, and send a sharp prick into his baby skin. Red blood pools, and I drip it onto the meter and hold him there while I ready the shot. He grabs my cheeks with both hands as the needle enters his thigh, and he pinches me just as hard as he can. I feel his fingernails in my cheeks, I feel them breaking through the skin underneath the hot tears running down, I feel the sting of the salt, and still, I let him pinch me. I am hurting him. He has every right to hurt me back. When the shot is empty, I set him down on the floor so I can get his lunch, and he runs up the stairs, runs down the hallway, runs into his room, and slams the door.

I sit down in the middle of the tile on my kitchen floor and weep.

You can't explain health to a three-year-old. You can't explain that you making him bleed three times a day, four times a day, eight times a day is keeping him alive. There is no logic in the tiny mind of a young boy who doesn't understand why his mother wants to hurt him, keeps hurting him, a mother who will continue to hurt him every day for the rest of his life. I sob. There is nothing else to do but cry.

I clean all of his favorite foods out of the pantry. The strawberry milk mix, the chocolate chips for the cookies we used to make every three days, and I think to myself that there won't be cookies anymore. On his birthday he chooses cake for dinner instead of a hot dog and a bun, because he isn't allowed to have both. We trade his Halloween candy in for a toy, and he likes the toy for one day, but the next day he wants his candy back, he wants his life back, *I want my life back.*

It has been a year of this life we don't want. I live in darkness. I have forgotten what it is to laugh. This is not mothering, not the mother I want to be. I am failing at everything. We pull into a parking space at a place I can't recall, but what I can recall is exactly what Greg says to me before he opens the door and steps out. "When are you ever going to come back?"

I walk around to the back of the car and tell him what I have become resigned to. "I might not." And it is true. I don't know how to get myself out of this dark place.

It is weeks after that question and my answer behind the car. I pull the insurance card out of my brown leather wallet and turn it over. It is still there on the back of the white card: the number to call if you are in need of mental health help. And I wonder if that is what this is. Because this person who I am is not who I used to be, and I don't want to be this person anymore. So I dial the number, and it rings, and a woman answers the phone. I am desperate; I don't think through the fact that it is a paid receptionist who is answering, and I pour out my heart, every aching part of it, into her waiting ears. When I am done, after it has all come spilling out, the fact that my life, and my personality, and my ability to cope have all been turned upside down, she answers. "Oh, honey," she says, "you just need a massage."

This is years ago, years before people got massages on a regular basis, and I am not sure what a massage even is, where I would get one, *why I would get one.* My whole life has been turned upside down, and this woman assures me that a one-hour massage will be the answer. I hang up the phone and realize I will live like this for the rest of my life. That phone call? That was my last resort. It took all of my courage to dial the number on the back of my health insurance card. The reality that I had been trying to avoid stares back at me, unfaltering. *This is my life.*

That night I tuck the boys into their beds. I pull the blue and green comforters up and they are cozy and warm, and I long for their quiet, peaceful sleep. I snuggle my daughter Megan as I rock her in the rocking chair. Her calm breathing calms my troubled heart, and when she has settled completely, I gently lay her in the waiting crib. I say good night to Greg, hear him roll over, hear the steady breathing begin. I have learned that these times, these are the best times to cry. The times when nobody knows. So they don't have to be frightened, so they don't carry the weight, so that in the daylight they might think things are getting better.

I lie motionless in my bed and stare at the ceiling as the tears run from the corners of my eyes and into the flannel pillowcase. I try to think through all the people in my life—surely there must be someone who would know how to help me get out of this place, this dark place, this place where I don't want to be. For an hour I cry and I think through the names of every single person I know. Surely there is someone. But at the end I take a deep, sob-racked breath and I realize what I have known all along. I am alone in this. I am alone.

I have been here before. Why is it that even with all of the learning, I am blind to the Lord again?

We Can't Make It Out of This

Whenever I come across the pages of 2 Kings, I pause to read chapter six. One of my favorite stories is here, and every time I visit this chapter it becomes real to me again. In my imagination, I am the servant in Dothan in the house within the city walls, and I don't realize yet that horses and chariots and a great host have surrounded us. We are compassed about, they are intent on destroying us, and I don't know.

I wake early in the morning, thinking we will sneak out before the danger comes, preparing to get out, but my eyes rise to the window and I see them there, see the army surrounding us, and the reality of it settles in. We can't make it out of this. We won't.

I wake my master and tell him. "Alas, my master! how shall we do?" He answers calmly, more calmly than I feel he should in this kind of situation, this desperate situation. "Fear not: for they that be with us are more than they that be with them" (2 Kings 6:15–16).

It is not true. I do not trust that it is true. My eyes do not lie; I see the reality before us. I see the horses and chariots,

I see the host, and we are in trouble here. We can't get out of this place; we won't get out. All is darkness, a weight pressing in, the burden suffocating; I resign myself to the reality of this. And then Elisha begins to pray: "Lord, I pray thee, open his eyes, that he may see" (2 Kings 6:17). Before the prayer is over, the light floods in. I open my eyes and I see. The mountain is full of horses and chariots of fire. God has not forgotten us. There in that dark place, the mountain burns with fire, and I see that it is true: we are surrounded by heaven's help. We have been all along.

Instead of rejoicing, I am filled with remorse. *Why did I not see it?*

What was it that held me back from the realization?

The truth sinks in and weighs on me; I am heavy with guilt. I am the servant. I am blind. And the biggest curse of this blindness is not the unseeing. It is the untrusting.

Is this how I enter every situation in my life?

Blind?

The question catches me unaware, and I determine to come to the resolution of it. I know I must find the answer if I am going to learn to trust God. I have walked the path that led me to discover how His goodness is evidence of His love, but what is it that will teach me how to trust? The answer can only be found in the asking of it, in the vulnerability of it. There is no escaping it now, and so I begin to consider.

Where is my blindness?

The walls come slamming down like floodgates, and I am not surrounded by horses and flaming chariots; I am flooded with the crashing-down reality that my blindness, my wall of distrust, may be more powerful than I had let myself believe. It has the power to hold me back; it could cause me to eventually walk away, to turn away from God, if I am not careful.

I see it there in my unmet expectations. How I worry that God will disappoint me. I am blind to the reality that His choice could be choicer, His ending could be endless, His best could be better than anything I could ever imagine. So I set up my finish line, I design my happy ending, I map out my Promised Land. I'm not sure I trust Him to do it, so I will set the expectation for my happiness. When the expectation is not realized, when the happy ending doesn't come in

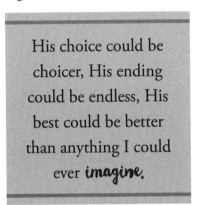

His choice could be choicer, His ending could be endless, His best could be better than anything I could ever *imagine.*

my way, in my timing, I am disappointed. I am disappointed in my life, and my reality, and my God.

Is it because I am blind?

I can see it in my fear. I know exactly what I am afraid of. If I give this to God, *completely* to God, I can't trust what the outcome will be. The person will die, we'll lose the house, the answer will take too long, I won't be strong enough. I am paralyzed by this fear, debilitated by it.

Is it because I am blind?

I see it in what I feel I am owed. I say my prayers. I serve the poor, the homeless, the neglected. I go to church. I read the scriptures. I keep the commandments. I am good to God; I am good *for* God. Shouldn't He be good to me? I don't want

Him to feel obligated to bless me, but if I do things His way, shouldn't I expect Him to sometimes do things my way? Not all the time, *I'm not asking for things to go my way all the time,* but surely some of the time. Is that too much to ask?

It is my bitterness in these moments that blinds me.

I realize that at the very root of all of this distrust is a desire to be in control. This is my life, I am in the trenches of it, I am living the reality of it, and I know what I need, what would be best. I know how things should work out. I already know. And it frustrates me to wait on God. I see how things should go—give me this promotion, let this doctor have the answer, remove this struggle from me, take away this illness, make it so that never happened, send the right person into my life. It would all be better, my life would be better, if He would just listen. If He would do it my way.

I think I am in control, and I am blind because of it.

It doesn't take long before I realize the truth. Maybe I am not looking for a God; maybe I want a butler. I stop dead in my tracks and I wonder about this. Do I really want an authentic relationship with God? Because that relationship will require defining our roles—knowing who God is and knowing who I am. The thought of it humbles me.

I feel safer when I am in charge of my life. I want to work out the details. I want to settle on what the promise, and the miracle, and the happy ending should be. In every situation, I already know what I am going to do, and *at least I'm doing something about it.* But if I give this, *even this,* fully to God—honestly, I'm not sure what God's going to do with it. I don't trust what He's going to do. I have to be in charge of this.

EVEN THIS

I don't know if I can walk away from that. *Can I really walk away from that?* Will I walk away from that?

In order to trust, I am going to have to let that go.

There is something terrifying about letting God be God.

A Prayer for Protection

I close my eyes and focus on soaking up the warmth of the sun. It is halftime, and I am exactly where I most love to be: on the sideline, cheering on my girls and their coach. This is my joy.

Just before the game is about to resume, I hear the prompting. *Pray for protection for Meg.* My heart begins to beat a little faster, but I rest in gratitude for the prompting. I will. I begin to pray. And every few minutes for the rest of the half, I continue that prayer. For protection. For Meg.

It is in the last two minutes of the game that it happens. Meg comes around the back of the goal intent on defending it. Her cleats move quickly across the turf, her lacrosse stick raised. She rushes the goal just as the opponent shoots, releasing the ball in one fluid motion, sending it flying toward the left corner of the net. It happens so fast that I can't see where the ball went; I just see Meg collapse on the ground.

The referees run over. They yell frantically for the coach, their arms beckoning in urgency. I watch Greg run from the coach's box and kneel down at our daughter's side and then hear him yelling for me to grab the keys. I watch him scoop Meg up in his arms, how he cradles her against his body as he begins to run. I follow, trying to catch up, adrenaline coursing through my veins. Keys in hand. Pain shooting through my heart. *Why did the protection not come? Why? Why, God?*

I look Meg over carefully when we get in the car. Her left eye is swollen beyond recognition. Where soft lashes would normally rest on smooth skin, I see her bruised and reddened skin stretched tight. A huge mass swells where her eye would normally be, as if a golf ball has been inserted underneath. She is in intense pain, and we drive the two blocks to where the hospital waits, just down the street from the high school field.

We enter the emergency room and the medical staff takes over, using sophisticated machinery to assess the damage. Bright lights. Blue gloves. Meg whimpering in pain. I try to chase the bitterness from my heart. Why did He not hear my prayer? Why send the prompting if it wasn't going to be answered? I feel the anger rush in with the fear, the doubt settling in thick. There is no trusting here.

Finally, Meg is calm. The doctor walks in from looking at the reports and sits on the round black stool to talk to Greg and me. "She is really lucky," he says. "A quarter inch lower and it would have shattered her cheekbone; a quarter inch higher and it would have damaged her eye; a quarter inch to the left and it would have hit a major artery—she could have been killed." He paused for a moment and then said the words I will never forget. "Your daughter was miraculously protected."

And for some reason, I had first turned to doubt.

The God I Believe In

Out of the five books in Lamentations, three of them begin with the word *how*. The chapters all start with a question, biblically phrased, but the veiled meaning of each is clear. *How did this happen? How could You have forgotten us? How could You allow bad things to happen to good people, Your people, Your chosen people?* The book is written from captivity, the captivity Jeremiah prophesied would last for seventy years. That is a lifetime for some people, and I wonder how you can learn to trust the One who wants you to spend a lifetime in captivity.

But God defines even this; He spells it out for them, what this captivity could look like. Build houses, and plant gardens, and have children, and let your children be married and welcome their children into this world, into these homes. Find peace in the city. "In the peace thereof shall ye have peace" (Jeremiah 29:7).

There is a lesson here, in the unreasonable assumption that contentment could be found in captivity. Maybe God was trying to help them recognize the goodness, even there, to remember that what is most important in any life—family, home, love—can be found anywhere. Even within captivity.

I drive down the dirt road that leads to the dump in the middle of Tijuana, Mexico, and my heart hopes that Javier will still be there. I walk up the stairs of the Church of God, past the wooden cross built out of two-by-fours, and throw open the brown door as I call out his name. When I find him he always asks me the same thing in his broken English. "Are you here for to bless?"

I answer the same way I always do. "Yes, I am here for to bless." Javier puts on his black apron in the church kitchen, and as we cook over the huge stove he teaches me to say "*Dios te bendiga*" God bless you. Just after the sun rises the people begin to walk in. For most, this will be the only meal they will eat today. We serve up the food on plastic plates; today's meal is eggs and beans. The people who come in eat it quickly and then head off to work, to school, to wherever they will go until this time tomorrow, when they will come back through here again. It isn't long before Javier's wife walks in with their seven small children, holding their infant son close, and I smile at the dark tuft of soft hair beneath the yellow blanket he is wrapped within.

We stop our work to celebrate this new baby, and the mother carefully places him in my arms so she can feed the others. Rocking him gently, I look outside the window at all of the squatter shacks there and then back into the small church kitchen where Javier's children are eating the one meal they will eat today, the only meal they will eat today, and I focus on their smiles and their love, and I realize that somehow they have found it. The peace of the city. Javier will cook and serve this breakfast to all of the other families in the dump this morning, the same way he does every morning. "Today is my day to bless," he explains. I find myself in awe of Javier's ability to serve with so much peace and joy.

Today is my day to **bless**.

Once all have been fed and the dishes are washed and the floor is swept, we prepare to go. He says it to me again, the way he always does, every time I leave, "*Dios te bendiga,*" and the truth of it pricks my heart. Compared to Javier's life, I have everything. *I have too much.* And yet, I do not live with the same peace Javier does. I wonder why.

The peace that the children of Israel were supposed to find in the midst of captivity did not come easily. The lack of it is what makes up most of the book of Lamentations. I love how chapter three begins: "I am the man who has seen affliction" (Lamentations 3:1). And that is all of us. It is you. It is me. I have seen affliction. I am that man. Chapter three is filled with this man's discontent. No, more than discontent. It is filled with anger and with bitterness. I read, and as I read I make a list of how the people living in captivity describe God. Surely He is *against me*; He turned His hand against me all the day. He has built against me and surrounded me with *bitterness*. He set me in *dark* places. He put a hedge completely around me. *There is no way out for us.* He made my chain heavy. When I cry out to Him, even when I shout, He shuts out my prayer, *He doesn't listen.* He is *uncaring.* He has made my paths crooked. There is no direction. He is like a bear lying in wait, a lion crouching in secret places; He waits to attack. He has bent His bow and made me a mark for the arrow. I am filled with bitterness, and He is the one who has made me bitter. He has removed my soul from peace. I don't even remember what prosperity is, my mind is filled with the memory of this misery, and it has made me bitter.

I look back over the words that fill those verses; I write them out on a piece of paper where I can see them. I fill up the sheet with accusations. *Against. Rejected. Mean. Bitter. Forgetful. Enslaved. Uncaring. Attacked. Forgotten. No guidance. Apathetic.* And I ask myself, *is this the God I believe in?*

I want to say no, but I am ashamed to admit I have felt that way before. There have been times that have led me to believe God has forgotten me. That He hasn't wanted the best for me. I don't have to look far to see the unfairness of life, how she lost her daughter while the child in the next room lived. How he got the promotion and the other man is homeless. How my children eat three meals a day and Javier's children eat just once, a plate filled with powdered eggs mixed with powdered milk, and that is the only thing they will eat that day, and they are happy.

And I don't know why they are so happy.

Why do they continue to trust this God who it seems has continually failed them? Why have they not become bitter against God?

It is later in the third chapter of Lamentations that I find the remedy, why Javier is so happy, why he feels so blessed.

> *This I recall to my mind, therefore have I hope.*
> *It is of the Lord's mercies that we are not con-*
> *sumed, because his compassions fail not.*
> *They are new every morning: great is thy faith-*
> *fulness.*
> *The Lord is my portion, saith my soul; therefore*
> *will I hope in him.*
> *The Lord is good unto them that wait for him, to*
> *the soul that seeketh him.*
> *It is good that a man should both hope and*
> *quietly wait for the salvation of the Lord.*
> *(Lamentations 3:21–26)*

I see this hope in Javier. I see how he has learned to recognize the mercy and the compassion of the Lord, how he sees it daily. And as He has traced the pattern of mercy and compassion, He has learned to trust that God is faithful. Javier lives in hope, quietly waiting, trusting that God will provide. I see his trust. It is evident to me.

I begin a new list to describe God on my paper. I take the words from those later verses in chapter three. *Hopeful. Merciful. Compassionate. Faithful. My portion. Good.*

Yes, this is the God I believe in.

This is the God I trust.

The End of the Story

I was the mother of a three-year-old whose life had been turned upside down. You remember how I lay motionless in my bed that night, staring at the ceiling as the tears ran down from the corners of my eyes and into the flannel pillowcase. The night when I realized again that I was alone.

Well, the story didn't end there. In fact, this is when the learning began.

I have been in this alone place before, so this time it isn't long before the realization settles in. I am not alone in this. *He knows.* God knows. I am certain of this. So I begin to pray, and even though He already knows everything, I start at the very beginning and I tell Him all of it. How much it hurts, how heavy the burden is that I carry daily, how exhausted I am from the weight of it. As I pour out my heart, I pray for the relief that is promised in Matthew 11: "Come unto me, all ye that labour and are heavy laden, and I will give you rest. Take my yoke upon you, and learn of me; for I am meek and lowly in heart: and ye shall find rest unto your souls" (Matthew 11:28–29). The tears continue to fall, and I plead with Him for this rest.

For the first time in so many months, I feel peace. It enters the room quiet, but thick, the comfort of it settling soft. I stop praying; I rest in the peace. All night long I rest in the peace. The next morning I pick up the burden and prepare to begin again, but this time I notice it is lighter. With time I learn that what will get me through the day, each dark day, is knowing the night will come, and with it the opportunity to pour out my heart in prayer again. To rest in Him. Those nighttime conversations become the balm that carries me through.

Years go by, and Josh is twelve. His diabetes has become a way of life. We are used to it—as used to it as we can be. Josh and I have been asked to participate in a research study at the University of Utah. They are following adolescents who have diabetes. It is a four-year study. They want to see how having this disease will affect Josh, how it will affect us. Being there makes me remember our reality.

I am in one room with a social worker, and Josh is in another. We each have a test in front of us, filled with multiple-choice questions. The test will take at least an hour to complete. I begin the questions, and they are easy, and I think that I will finish faster than they expect. But then I get to one question I can't answer, and I pause. I sit there for a long time before the social worker finally asks if I need help.

"I don't know if I can answer this question," I tell her. I have been struggling with it for ten minutes, and I can't decide how to respond.

"It's all right," she assures me. "Just initial it so we know you read it and you can leave it blank."

But I can't. I have to figure out the answer. The unknowing doesn't sit well with me.

The question says, "If you knew it meant you would have to give up all of the learning, would you choose to never have had your child diagnosed with diabetes?"

Of course the right answer is yes. It's so easy. I shouldn't even have to think about it. But *all of the learning*—that is the part that holds me back.

I think about the conversations Josh and I have had. Because of this, he has learned to have empathy for those who are different, his heart goes out to the one; he is known for this. I think of how he holds on to the verse in Joshua, "Be strong and of a good courage" (Joshua 1:9) He thinks it was written for him; he has thought that since he was three. I think of how he has learned to lean on Jesus, to find strength in Him.

As I look back I realize that this learning hasn't only been good for Josh.

I remember those late nights in my bedroom, the conversations that I looked forward to during those dark days, the moments when I poured out my heart in prayer to Him. I remember the peace, the way the burden seemed to be lighter every morning, and I realize I can't give those memories up. Those late nights, those intimate moments when I had learned to trust God, were too precious to me. And I realize the truth I never thought I would arrive at.

I am not willing to give up the learning.

It dawns on me that sometimes the places of deepest hurt

> You only *trust* Him as deeply as you *need* Him.

allow us to forge the bonds of deepest trust. I am reminded of the scripture in Psalms, "Deep calleth unto deep" (Psalm 42:7). It's true. You only trust Him as deeply as you need Him. And I needed Him in this. Desperately needed Him. I called to Him from the depths of despair, and He gave me reason to trust.

Yet the Lord will command his lovingkindness in the daytime,
and in the night his song shall be with me,
and my prayer unto the God of my life.
(Psalm 42:8)

Taking the Yoke

It is the yoke in Matthew 11 that I am focused on now. If I take the yoke, I will find rest. That is the promise. I know about that rest; I have experienced it; it is real to me. But I don't understand what it has to do with the yoke.

I am riding down a street lined with tall poplar trees in a carriage pulled by a matching pair of oxen. I watch the muscles strain under their buttercream coats, and I am fascinated by the way they move as one, turn as one, pull as one. The wooden yoke hangs evenly across their backs, allowing them to support the weight of the carriage equally. Instinctively each knows what the other will do. They know the other will support his share of the weight. They trust each other.

I see it, but I still don't understand—what does the yoke have to do with rest?

I am reminded of my grandma's crystal vase, the one I took out of the cupboard it is usually stored in so I could use it more often. I remember the day I walked around the house after filling it with dusty pink roses, searching for the place it would sit. I looked at the solid cream shelf hanging above the chest of drawers in the family room. It would be beautiful there. But the shelf hangs crooked. It always has. I cannot *rest* the vase on that shelf, because I do not trust the strength of it.

It is in that instant that the meaning of the verse hits me with full force. I cannot rest on something I don't trust.

The yoking becomes the trusting. Taking the yoke means I have allowed my heart to trust in Him, that I have let go of what holds me back—the fear, the unmet expectation, the control. I let it all go when I take up the yoke. I agree to move in the direction He wants to move. To turn the corners He wants to turn. To pull whatever weight He sees fit for me to pull. *With* Him.

It is within that trusting place that I will find rest.

Perhaps you have already found this rest.

But maybe you fear that you don't match up to the Lord. You hear Him extend the invitation, "Take my yoke," but you know it is not meant for you. You are not a perfectly matched partner. You cannot pull an equal weight. You are the weak one. *I am the weak one.* I know that fear.

We sit together on a black leather couch and I hold a bundle of white, wadded tissues in my lap. I have poured out the truth of it—how my life was perfect until my wedding day, until we were married. Then everything went downhill. For ten years life has gone downhill. The tumor, the diabetes, the unnumbered miscarriages, the babies we never held out-numbering the ones we did. The exhaustion that came with the four pregnancies we barely made it through. The months and months of bed rest. The years without pay, without a job, without steady income. We have borne the weight of it. We are tired, Greg and I; we are worn out.

I see the wisdom in the counselor's eyes as he looks us over, appraises us, and I wonder what counsel he will give. But the words he has for us do not contain advice. Instead he begins to tell us about an auction, a farmer's auction, where people are buying pigs and sheep and oxen. They file into the arena to be sold, each owner entering with his livestock, and the oxen enter the arena last. They are brought into the arena in matching pairs, yoked together, ready to pull. Each team is harnessed to the heavy load in the middle of the arena, and before the auctioning begins, they pull the load forward. When they are done, the auctioneer begins his calling, and the numbers are raised, one after the other until each team is sold. The teams come out in order. Those who can pull the most weight are saved for last. The longer the night wears on, the more beautiful the pairs become—matching height, matching weight, even the color of their coats matching.

Finally, the auctioneer calls for the last team to be brought out. An old man enters the arena before the pair. The farmer, stooped with age, stands calm. His team follows behind. As they enter the ring a murmur moves through the crowd. People begin to scoff. Some laugh out loud. One ox is huge, by far the biggest ox that has entered the arena that evening. His legs are powerful, his shoulder muscles hardened with use; the yoke barely finds room to rest just behind his massive head. The other ox pales in comparison. The animal is small and scrawny. It looks malnourished. Not only is it dwarfed by its counterpart, the yoke hangs heavily across its back. The farmer harnesses them to the load and then adds more weight. More weight than any team has pulled so far. Then he calls to the oxen to move. With one accord they begin the work of it, moving in sync, fluid, each one making up for the weakness of the other, pulling the heavy load. A hush fills the stadium seats. The unexpectedness of it leaves the spectators in awe. And then the auctioneer begins to call; one by one the numbers are raised. The team sells for the highest price of any team that evening.

I hear the story and I know who I am. I am the scrawny one. The one you think will struggle. The one who is having trouble pulling her weight. *I am the weakest one.* And for some reason the Lord has agreed to be yoked with me. The idea of it brings me to my knees. He will have to pull harder, lead stronger, push on longer because of my weakness, and still He extends the invitation. "Take my yoke."

Where Was God?

I stand in the middle of a cobblestone road just east of Church Street in downtown Charleston. This is it; this is the one place I wanted to make sure we stopped while we were here. I step up off the rocky thoroughfare and onto a paved sidewalk. There is no rhyme or reason to the paving, each slate haphazardly placed with no regard for color, pattern, or size. It's all thrown together, even the broken pieces set in, the mortar barely holding. All of it is falling apart.

Lifting my eyes, I look up at the wrought-iron letters nailed into the cement. MART. There is no adornment, no fancy architecture here, just the four letters made permanent on the gray wall. I walk in through the glass doors and look around the warehouse structure at the dull brick and gray cement, and I try to imagine the stories these walls would whisper if they could share the horror that took place here.

Had I walked through this door a century and a half ago, I would have seen benches set up in front of a platform, and just beyond that, a four-story brick building with gated windows and iron doors. Yes, all those years ago this was a prison yard and an auction house, where whippings took place and doses of salt were poured into open wounds. A place where people, living and breathing people, were sold like commodities. Men and women in shackles, infants stripped from arms, brothers and sisters torn apart. In the year 1859, what could no longer be done on city corners took place in darkened warehouses, where thousands of beautiful lives, each God's masterpiece, were sold as property.

The injustice of it leaves me without words. I think of Jeremiah's people, sent into captivity for seventy years to build homes, and plant gardens, and have children, and their experience pales in comparison. The men, women, and children taken from this building were stripped from their families, they worked other people's gardens, they never built homes.

I leave the slave market and drive to a plantation to hear the story of how they lived, how they worked, how they survived. I stand in front of a cotton gin and listen to the history, but I am not as captivated by it as I am by the black man who stands next to me, listening to the details, his blue African dashiki gently moving in the breeze. I watch him walk up to the old red wall of the cotton gin and scan the bricks carefully for the two fingerprints left all those years ago by a slave whose job was to turn each one. Finding it, he raises his hand slowly to the red brick, and I watch how he presses his two fingertips into the prints, how he holds them there as he ponders.

There is part of me that wants to ask what he is thinking, but I don't. I watch him in silence. I tune out the tour guide, who is repeating memorized details of history, and I focus intently on the man who is reliving it. These are his people, and he has heard this story told time and time again, from his father, and his father's father. He tells me this later, as we stand outside the whitewashed slave shacks under the oak trees just down the lane from the main house.

"Where was God in this?" I ask him after the tour has dissipated. He has lingered there, and so have I, because I have finally gathered enough courage to ask for the insight that won't be found in the tour guide's notes.

"Hmmmm." He looks at me to see if my heart is honest, and then he begins to speak. "It was my grandmother who told me how she would look at the main house and question God. 'The same God who hears their prayers, why doesn't He hear mine?' It took her time to come to terms with that," he told me. "Time and learning."

Just believe and trust. Everything will come in its *time*.

"Joe," she used to tell him, "we just believe and trust. Everything will come in its time. In time. In time." He stops, as if considering it, and then continues.

"I am a firm believer of this," he says. "Weeping may endure for the night, but joy comes in the morning" (see Psalm 30:5).

He talks about the slaves and tells me that they didn't work from sunup to sundown, but from "I can" to "I can't."

"Yes," he says, "they worked from 'I can' until 'I can't no longer,'" and I imagine them coming home after the long day's work to the small white shacks with small brick fireplaces, ten of them squished into one tiny shack, falling asleep on the hard wood floor without dinner. But that isn't how it went, he tells me. When evening came, they would meet at the river and encourage each other with song. The singing brought the Spirit, and that was their respite and their relief.

"Oh, ya," he says it slow, the Gullah accent thick on his tongue. "If we had been here then, we would have seen glimpses of joy and laughter mixed in between the hollering and cracking of whips. And through it all we would have heard the singing."

In a strong, deep voice, he begins to sing. It is unexpected, unanticipated, and I feel my heart leaning into the warmth and richness of his voice. We stand under the oak trees next to the brick steps of the small white shack, me in silence, and him singing the song his grandmother taught him. If I were to close my eyes, I think perhaps I would see them there covered in dust and sweat, walking in from the fields, wondering if there would be any dinner tonight, and filling the evening air with song.

> *Well, now I looked over Jordan, and what did*
> *   I see?*
> *Comin' for to carry me home.*
> *There was a band of angels a-comin' after me,*
> *Comin' for to carry me home.*
>
> *Swing low, sweet chariot,*
> *Comin' for to carry me home.*
> *Swing low, sweet chariot,*
> *Comin' for to carry me home.*
>
> *Well, I'm sometimes up and I'm sometimes down,*
> *Comin' for to carry me home.*
> *But I know my soul is heavenly bound,*
> *Comin' for to carry me home.*

Swing low, sweet chariot,
Comin' for to carry me home.
Swing low, sweet chariot,
Comin' for to carry me home.

I walk across the grounds, underneath the oak trees, toward the cemetery where his people are buried, and I let the words penetrate my soul. *That same God who hears you, why doesn't he hear me?* They would work from "I can" to "I can't no longer." In the waiting there was always the singing. We just have to believe and trust. Everything will come in its time. In time. In time. There is wisdom in those fragments. Gold, tried in the fire. God, tried in the fire.

I lean into the learning that comes from the stories of those who have no reason to trust, and still do—the ones who live through trials where most would choose bitterness and instead choose to forge ahead in faith. I want it to sink in, what Joe taught me about holding on to God. I want his story to enlarge my heart, to stretch the capacity of my soul's understanding.

The sun is setting; the rays slant yellow across the plantation, touching everything with light. Joe stands there, under the boughs of the old oak tree, his hand-carved walking stick in one hand, the small wooden cross hanging crooked from the top. I look back, and he is the last thing I see.

THE REFLECTING PLACE

This season of life has found me repeating the scripture found at the end of Matthew 11 over and over again. "Come unto me, all ye that labour and are heavy laden, and I will give you rest. Take my yoke upon you, and learn of me; for I am meek and lowly in heart: and ye shall find rest unto your souls. For my yoke is easy, and my burden is light" (Matthew 11:28–30).

I can't help but wonder about the ease of this yoke. I begin a study. It is as I turn to the Greek translation that the meaning becomes clear. The Greek word for "easy" is *chrestos*. It can be translated as useful, better, gracious, kind, and good—as in goodness. I hold on to the word *goodness*.

"Come unto me, all ye that labour and are heavy laden. . . . Take my yoke upon you . . . for my yoke is *goodness,* and my burden is light."

It is the end of the day, and I spend a moment in reflection as I have been doing for months now. This is where I trace God's love. It has become a necessity, an end-of-day ritual; a soothing that comes before the slumber. It is the pattern of my life, but tonight I will add a second piece. Tonight I will add something new.

After I trace the goodness and express gratitude, I will look back over the day through the moments that someone else might overlook, and I will try to pinpoint the times when I have faltered. The times when fear took over, when I let the

bitterness of unmet expectations begin to rise, when I wanted to retake control. I will focus on the moments when I failed to trust. I will acknowledge them, and once I have recognized my mistake in them, I will let them go.

The exercise is powerful, and I decide I will keep doing this. Every single night after I trace the goodness of His love, I will reflect on the times that have distanced me from God, and I will let them go. It is my way of taking up the yoke.

Tracing the goodness and expressing my gratitude.

Reflecting on my weakness and letting go.

In the process, I am learning what it is to trust.

Let Go of What Holds You Back

Keeping God at Arm's Length

There is a part of my heart that wonders—has just begun to wonder—if maybe there is another side to this. Could it be that because I have been so afraid, so busy pushing God away, I am living beneath God's privilege for me? What if there is a well—a reservoir of blessings—that I have not yet approached because I have been so careful about keeping God at arm's length?

Maybe on purpose.

Maybe unintentionally.

Either way, I have been doing that.

I am weak in this, humbled. Ready to live life differently.

The looking forward presses down on me. It is uncertain. I do not know what lies ahead. There are questions that I must wrestle with, questions that will lead to deeper answers, to a different path. Sometimes I fear giving something up because of what I might lose. I know this about myself. It is this fear that paralyzes me at times. And yet, I am coming to believe that if I choose God's path, what lies in front of me will always be better than what I am leaving behind. I lean

> If I choose God's path, what lies in front of me will always be *better* than what I am leaving behind.

into the hard questions and wait for the answers that I know will follow. What will my journey look like if I trust God with my whole heart? What if I don't approach life by leaning on my own understanding? Is it possible that God holds in His hands blessings I can't even begin to anticipate? That He is patiently waiting for me to ask for the miracle He has designed rather than the one I have?

I consider the truth of this and make a decision.

Maybe letting go will allow me to take hold of the miracle that is already within my reach.

Understanding Why Sometimes He Doesn't

Making Sense of the Holes

When we all gather around the table for dinner, that is when my heart is most happy. My eyes move from person to person and I rediscover contentment. Not just with the act of gathering—I am content with *who* we have gathered. This new set of family that has joined our home, the ones born into our family through marriage—I love them. My eyes travel around the table and linger on my oldest son, Caleb, *the wise one.* He and Maria will leave for Nebraska within the next few months, and a part of my heart will go with them. I look over at Joshua, *who is my strength.* Even sooner, he and Janaye will drive to Texas, and a part of my heart will journey with them there. Garett is next, *my understanding;* in January he and Natalie will welcome a little one into the world. I am beyond myself with the excitement of it; already I feel my heart starting to expand. Then Grace, *my miracle,* she is the one who will keep the nest from becoming empty for just a while longer. Oh, how my heart is grateful for that. Last I look at Megan, who sits beside me, and her husband, J.J., who has just walked over to the table. Megan is *my joy.*

Born into the beginning of our tribulation with Josh, she has kept my heart happy. It is still true today. She is brilliant in book smarts, this one, but she has no common sense. We laugh about that, how she gets straight A's in school but also has more than her fair share of blonde moments. Yes, her lack of common sense has brought a lot of laughter over the years. Incidentally, sometimes the same is true of her new husband, and because of that I can't begin to tell you the joy their conversation brings to these family gatherings. We never know what either one of them is going to say.

Tonight is no different.

For months now, Megan has been complaining about their washer. It is ripping holes in their shirts. I tell her to run her fingers around the drum, looking for a sharp edge, but there is none. We talk about her detergent. We consider the dryer. All to no avail. Now she brings it up again. "Look, Mom, there is one of the holes I have been telling you about." I look closely and I can see it there just above the hem of his shirt. It is a tiny hole, the size of a pencil eraser. "It only happens to J.J.'s shirts," she tells me. "The holes are always in that same place."

This is going to be one of *those* moments, I can already tell. We wait for it, for the logic that makes perfect sense in her world, but absolutely none for the rest of us.

"Your dryer isn't that smart," I tell her. "It doesn't know how to tear a hole in the same place on every single one of J.J.'s shirts." We all consider this for a moment, and then Caleb offers a suggestion.

"Maybe it's his belt that's making the hole?" All of us begin to nod. The hole is right next to his belt buckle. That has to be it. Even J.J. nods, for a minute. Then he begins shaking his head from side to side.

"No," he says, "that's not it. We don't wash our belts."

The table erupts in laughter. There's that happy joy that is at its finest when we spend enough time with these two. Both brilliant, but both lacking common sense. It is at the same time endearing and entertaining. I don't know what we would do without them.

Perhaps we all have these moments in God's eyes. The moments when He holds complete understanding of the situation, and we are unable to grasp it. And sometimes it is funny, but oftentimes it is painful. When things don't make sense. When we don't understand. When what should have been clear isn't.

These are the moments when we long to understand what doesn't make sense to us at all.

A Miracle in the Making

At the beginning of the story of the dreamer with the coat of many colors, I don't see God. I read about brothers who hated a young boy for his dreams, but I don't read anything about God. And when I read of the day when the son followed his father's counsel and went to the place where his brothers fed the flock of sheep, I think to myself that he should have stayed back with his father. Where he was safe. Where he was protected. Yes, he should have just stayed home. But Joseph goes, and eleven brothers watch this hated dreamer coming, and they decide to throw him into a pit. An empty pit in the middle of the desert. The sun beats down hot on parched ground, and the dreamer has been thrown into a deep pit with no water.

I don't see God in the pit.

When the brothers decide to trade the dreamer in the pit for a bag of silver, I look for God again. Where was God when this boy was about to be taken away from his father's love, far away from home, taken into Egypt to be a slave, all because of a God-sent dream? Where was God then?

Surely, Joseph must have wondered.

I would have. I know exactly what I would have thought. *Why? Why, God?* I would have pled desperately for a miracle. A rescue. Deliverance. And just like Joseph, I would not have known that deliverance was the very miracle God had in mind, but the timing was wrong. God couldn't send that miracle when Joseph was in the pit. No, this was a miracle in the making.

Before long, Joseph is thrown into prison for something he didn't deserve. Into the dark, into despair. *Why does this keep happening?* There is a baker and a butler, dreams of wine in a cup and baskets of bread, and once again I read verses about the dreamer interpreting dreams. There, mixed in with the interpreting of dreams taking place inside the dark walls of the prison, I stumble on this verse: "The Lord was with Joseph" (Genesis 39:21).

Finally, I see God.

With the seeing comes some of the understanding I have been longing for. If the Lord was there with Joseph in the prison, He must have been with him in the palace. And if that is true then surely He was with him in the pit. My heart finds comfort in knowing that God was with the dreamer all along. I think to myself that God must have been listening to the pleading taking place within the prison. The pleading for a rescue, for deliverance, for the very miracle God already had in mind. But the timing was still wrong. So Joseph spent day after day within the dark walls of the prison he didn't deserve, and he waited, and God did not leave him. God was there during the waiting. Working. Orchestrating the miracle.

I know that waiting place. It is the place where I have

prayed for the miracle that seems reasonable to ask for. I have watched for it and pled for it through the changing seasons and the lengthening years, and I have wondered why. *Why is it taking so long?*

But it's not just the waiting that concerns me about this story. There is more—there is something else I do not understand. From the very beginning, God knew Joseph was a dreamer. He is the One who sent the dream that landed Joseph in the pit, in the palace, in the prison. Shouldn't that God-given gift have made Joseph's life easier? Instead, God's gift is what kept leading Joseph into the places he didn't want to go. That thought makes me stop reading every time I get to this part of the story. It is hard to understand. If Joseph was using his gift, why didn't God protect him from the hurt, from the heartache, from harm? Why would He give Joseph a gift that would take him away from his loved ones, from his home? Why was Joseph given a gift that seemed as if it would destroy him? A gift that seemed to be preventing Joseph from obtaining the miracle God had in mind? No, it doesn't make any sense at all.

Until the famine comes.

I read about the parched ground, the rain that doesn't fall, and I am reminded how Joseph was finally released from prison because of another dream. A dream about cows and corn. There is a ruler who believes, and a country that prepares, all because of Joseph's inspiration and foresight. And then I read about eleven brothers who come into Egypt looking for rescue. For deliverance. For the kind of miracle that was only possible because of the heaven-sent preparations of a dreamer. It was the miracle I had wanted for Joseph from the minute he was thrown into the pit, a miracle that had taken years to orchestrate, one that required sacrifice and pain, one that could come only after the waiting.

And what if God had sent the miracle to Joseph in the pit?

I understand now why He didn't. God had a greater miracle in mind. The dreamer is proof that God is working there in the waiting places. When it seems heaven is silent, that is when the grandest orchestration is taking place. This is a story meant to remind us that God forgets not His own and that when the details of life are beyond our understanding, we must learn to trust His.

> When the details of life are beyond our understanding, we must learn to *trust* His.

God knew from the very beginning that there would come a day when eleven brothers would journey into Egypt to find a miracle. Perhaps these brothers heard about the corn and the cows, the seven years of plenty and the seven years of famine. We don't know. But eventually, the brothers recognize that the dreamer who saved Egypt is Joseph. Their own brother. The boy they gave away.

So Joseph's brothers come pleading. They ask for his forgiveness. I watch Joseph closely; I want to see what he will do. It is his right to ask, "Why? Why the pit? Why the bag of silver in place of a brother? Why the years in prison?" But Joseph doesn't. Instead, he asks his brothers a question that changes my heart: "Am I in the place of God?" (Genesis 50:19).

I listen carefully, and I understand what he is saying. *In the end, isn't the place where I ended up after all of these trials the exact place God needed me to be?* I consider it. Had there not been the pit, the slavery, the years in prison, there would not have been the opportunity for leadership, for saving a nation, for saving his family. The truth of it is that the trials are what enabled Joseph to be in the exact place God needed him to be. To provide the rescue. To prepare for the deliverance. To orchestrate the miracle God had in mind from the very moment Joseph was thrown into the pit.

It is here, in this line, that the understanding comes: "As for you, ye thought evil against me; but *God meant it unto good,* to bring to pass, as it is this day, to save much people alive" (Genesis 50:20; emphasis added). Because he was a dreamer, Joseph was led to a place he didn't want to go, a place he surely prayed to get out of, a place that had the potential to destroy him. But God meant it unto good. God *turned it* unto good. It was because of the pit and the prison that the true majesty of God was revealed. His capacity for the miraculous. His glory.

Joseph would have missed it, all of the majesty and the miracles, if he would have just stayed home. The very purpose for the dreams would never have been realized.

It was a miracle in the making from the very first moment.

Sometimes we don't understand. Sometimes things don't make any sense. Sometimes God leads us into the place we don't want to go because He knows that it is only within that place that His true capacity for our good will be revealed.

Out of My Comfort Zone

The gray hangs low, the wind blows, the rain is falling. I am here, but I don't want to be. I want to be home, where it is warm, where it is dry. The youth activity was planned months ago, but nobody planned for this rain. We could have canceled, *we should have canceled,* but because it was written with ink on the calendar we have come. And so we hike under the tall canopy of green pines, over the thick carpet of brown needles, in the pouring rain. When we reach the outdoor amphitheater the lightning begins—flashes of white against the ominous gray. It is far away, but it won't be for long.

I think we should head back for home. Get out of the rain and the weather. It feels like the right thing to do. But I am not in charge of this activity. The camp host suggests that maybe we should move to the cover of a pavilion. So we do. I help move brown picnic tables into rows within the haven of the canopy above. We sit shoulder to shoulder for warmth. The boys try to start a fire just outside the structure, but the downpour is too daunting. The flames smother after every attempt. Finally, someone stands at the front to talk about Jesus. It is what we came here to do. We listen intently, trying to capture the soft rhythm of the young girl's voice over the downpour tapping its incessant rhythm on the roof above.

It is as the young girl finishes, just as she sits down at the closest picnic table, that the real show begins. It is almost as if her witness of Jesus was the opening act. Lightning lights up the black of the night sky, and a deafening clap of thunder follows close behind. The pine trees stand as a stark black outline to the glory taking place in the backdrop. The deep sound that follows every flash of light rumbles loudly between the mountain walls, eventually echoing into the stillness. We are mesmerized. With each flash of light, each clap of thunder, we soak up the glory of it. There, under the protection of the pavilion, we are witnessing firsthand the majesty of God. You might have thought we had come just for this—bought tickets and sat down in front-row seats for the performance taking place. It is better than the Fourth of July.

> We can't begin to understand the majesty of God unless we are *willing* to meet Him in a place where it can be made *manifest*.

I sit back and watch the glory I would have missed if I had been given my way. Because the comfort of my four-walled home, the protection of my roof, would have kept me from experiencing this majesty.

It is then that I grab hold of the understanding: some-times He leads us out of our comfort zone and into uncharted territory in order to show us the fullness of His glory. The truth of it settles deep into my heart—we can't begin to understand the majesty of God unless we are willing to meet Him in a place where it can be made manifest.

The Place I Didn't Want to Go

I am seventeen weeks pregnant when the complications begin. This is our fourth baby, so I recognize the contractions immediately when they start. For three days and three nights I time the constant rhythm and I worry. There have been complications with every pregnancy—with each of the three babies we held on to before this pregnancy, and with each of the pregnancies we lost. I know what these contractions mean. The chance of loss, the months of bed rest ahead. We have been through this before.

But the contractions have never come this early; I am barely four months along. I pray for them to end. I pray for God to calm their consistency. I try to have faith. But finally, I drive myself to the hospital. Greg stays home with the kids because we know how this will go. I will stay for two hours to be monitored, the nurses and doctor will come up with a plan, I will come home and get in bed and never get back up until the baby comes. Yes, I know how this will go.

But things don't go how I have planned.

I won't forget the nurse telling me that at seventeen weeks

I am not far enough along for them to offer any help, that the pregnancy isn't viable at this many weeks, that the tiny kicks inside my growing womb do not constitute a life that they are authorized to save. I sob. I explain how this pregnancy has been my most viable pregnancy so far, how I have never made it this many weeks without a complication. I beg the nurse to call my doctor. When she leaves the room, I lie still on the bed and listen to the constant beating of the tiny heart on the monitor. Through the tears I watch the lines tracking the contractions that are witness to the battle this child will have to fight against to live.

The nurse returns with words of promise: the doctor wants to treat this pregnancy as if it is viable. He confirms what I have already told her—this has been my most successful pregnancy thus far. We will fight to keep the baby. I return home to complete bed rest. For four weeks I lie still. I do not move. My body aches with the pressure of it all. It is as if I am keeping every muscle taut in order to hold the baby inside. I am worn out physically and emotionally, and still the contractions do not stop. I can't bear the thought of losing this baby. Of delivering a tiny girl that will be capable of taking only a few short breaths and will then pass away in my arms. I am not strong enough. I know I am not that strong.

But after four weeks, when it becomes apparent that the contractions are not going to stop even with the help of medication and bed rest, we meet with Dr. Brown. There is a surgery. It is risky at this point in the pregnancy. Either it will work, or we will lose the baby. He lays out the truth of it bare: we could lose the baby during the surgery. I might miss seeing the baby alive because I will not be awake. Again,

I sob. He feels it is our only hope. I wonder why it has to be so hard. *This good thing, this desire to bring new life into the world, why does it have to go like this?*

I lie on the bed in the middle of the operating room with a soft white blanket laid over my swollen belly. Underneath the warmth I slide my hands to rest on the roundness and try to feel the stirrings of life within. It might be the last moment I have with this tiny one. I know this. I don't pass up the opportunity to connect one last time. I am afraid, but even more than being afraid, I am exhausted. Too exhausted to pray, to beg for the life of this child, to ask for the success of this surgery. The anesthesiologist starts to count down from ten, and it is almost time. I am sliding into sleep, but before I do, I pray the only words of which I am capable: "Thy will be done; please bless us."

I wake in the recovery room. I feel myself sliding in and out of wakefulness. I see the anesthesiologist, feel him check the pulse in my wrist, watch him write something on his chart. It is hard to form words. I wrestle with trying to remember how to speak. But I have to know. "Did it work?" I ask him, my raspy voice a surprise to both of us. "Am I still pregnant?" I hear him whisper yes as I drift back off to sleep. Just before the sleep comes, I place my hand once again over the roundness, and a whisper settles into my heart. "Thanks be unto God for his unspeakable gift" (2 Corinthians 9:15).

I am on bed rest for four months, allowed to sit up for only ten minutes every day. Once a week I go to a doctor's appointment. I learn that when people don't see you around, they forget you exist. I spend hours every day by myself. My mother comes to pick up my children every morning and they return home with Greg every night. During the day, I am alone. No one stops by to visit. In the silence of it all, I turn to the one friend who is constant. I find Him in the Word. I speak to Him in prayer. Over the days that turn into weeks, and eventually into months, I pour out my heart to Him, I learn of Him, I rest in Him. He becomes for me courage, the promise of good things to come, my place of refuge, a constant source of strength. He is peace, hope when hope is gone, and my stronghold. With time, I realize that He has become more than just someone to believe in; He has become real to me. My understanding has deepened. I have proven Him, and He has been there.

It is after the five months of bed rest are over, after the six hours of labor. After the doctor holds Grace up in front of the nurses in the delivery room to tell them to look closely, for they are witnessing a miracle—this baby would not be here if it weren't for the faith of her mother. It is after we arrive home with our tiny baby girl with the soft white hair that I finally realize this truth: it was in the depths of the place that I didn't want to go that I was able to understand more clearly the capacity of God. His goodness. His realness. His love.

> Maybe the trial isn't always about God trying to prove *us* or build *our* character—what if He is trying to help us discover *His?*

If all had gone well I would not have gained that understanding.

I consider something I haven't ever thought of before. Maybe the trial isn't always about God trying to prove *us* or build *our* character—what if He is trying to help us discover *His?*

I wonder what He has allowed you to go through so you might understand Him better.

Longing for Understanding

For months he has been feeling it: an overwhelming prompting to quit his job. He can't shake it. Every single day he feels the prompting to leave. "I feel a prompting too," I tell him. "Mine says you shouldn't leave before you get a new job." But he doesn't listen to me. He follows the prompting. God's prompting. After months of wondering what to do, he turns in his resignation. We are jobless.

It will be okay, I tell myself. If God sent the prompting, surely He will send a job. But months go by without even an interview. Not one interview. We begin to worry. When we pray, we both receive the same answer: *God has something in mind for you; just wait.* But the answer doesn't make sense. And still, the months go by.

Our prayers become more desperate. *Please speed up the process; help us find the job You have in mind for us. Let us find the job this month, this week, tomorrow.* And still, the months go by.

Until finally we stumble on what surely is the answer. Everything falls into place. Within a week we go from being jobless to owning a small garage door company. We sign on the line; we use every bit of our remaining savings and then some. Greg begins working again. On the day we sign the papers, the woman who had previously owned the company shares her story. She tells us of how her husband had been diagnosed with cancer, how for the last six months he had worked the business every day, how they had prayed that the cancer would progress slowly. *Please slow down the process. Just give us one more month, one more week; just give us one more day.* And I remember our prayers, and I consider God, who watched from heaven and tried to balance the needs of these two families. In that defining moment I catch a glimpse of what it means to trust God's timing.

The new job feels heaven-sent.

We receive several confirmations that it is right for us, for our family. The confirmations are so undeniable that there is no doubting that this is what God has in mind for Greg to do.

But as the years go by it doesn't make sense. Every year we go deeper into debt, until finally we must get out, before this God-sent business completely devastates us financially. Greg finds another job. We move on, but not without a financial burden that will follow us for years.

And I wonder why. *Why, God?*

It's not that I can't trace goodness there. I can. I see it in the fact that Greg was able to give so much time to our church during those four years—time that became a sweet blessing for our family and for those he served. And I see the goodness that came for the eighteen-year-old boy we picked up off the street. The one who came to live with us unexpectedly after he had been in jail. The one who rode in the cab of the truck with Greg to fix garage doors day after day after day for eighteen months, because during those first days—those first months—it wasn't safe to leave the boy home alone. The conversations with Greg in the cab of that truck saved that boy's life. They gave him time to turn his life around, to get back on his feet. I know they did. To God, the cost of that boy's life was far greater than the debt we incurred. I get it.

But that doesn't make the questioning go away. I don't understand why it seems that God's answer cost us so dearly. I can't understand it.

I long for the understanding of that.

The Sand Dollar

The sand is a welcome home, and I greet it the same way I always do: by taking off my shoes. It is my signature, saying hello to the ocean in bare feet. I always have. I always will.

I walk down to the surf and face the great expanse of water head-on, eyes fixed on the horizon. I breathe, I still my heart, I let the ocean begin to mend what is broken in me, what is unsettled, what has been left unresolved since the last time I was here. It is my way.

It's been a hard season. Things are okay; we're okay. But sometimes I feel disillusioned by the way life has turned out. If I let myself think about it, the weight of it makes me sad. When I look at it closely, in the quiet moments, I remember the ache of it. The remembering leads me to pick up my on-going conversation with God.

The ocean is my favorite place to pray. It always has been. I start just where I left off with the conversation, the one I never end with *amen,* the conversation that just continues on. He is used to this by now. He knows this about me. We go back to the same things I have been praying about for days, for weeks, for months. To the unresolved questions that have filled my prayers for some time now. Years, even. I still need the same questions answered. We need to fix some things. He knows. *He knows.* I have a whole check-list of things God needs to take care of, and He already knows all of them. I bring them up every single time. I wonder how He never tires of me. Of my asking. How He welcomes the continuation of the prayer that has filled my life.

What do you need *God* to be?

I walk, and I pray. The wet, foamy sand massages my toes, the gentle surf making its presence known in a rhythm that covers my feet and then retreats, again and again, soothing my soul. I remind Him of the unresolved things. I address each one in detail. I pause in between to make sure I've said it just right, laid out the want in detail. Forgetting nothing. It is during one of these pauses that a question settles itself into my heart.

What do you need God to be?

The question catches me off guard. It is one I have never considered before. It would have made more sense if the question had been *what do you need God to do?* That's easy. In fact, I have a whole list. My to-do list for God. I think of the list, I go over it my head; I think how the items on the list won't work for this new question.

What do you need God to be?

I begin to consider it. For a minute I don't even know where to start; I haven't looked at things through this lens before. I have to think deeply about this. I focus on the horizon again, I breathe, I still my heart, and I begin.

I would need God to be great. Greater than this. Bigger than the problem that has consumed so much of our life. It's bigger than us; I am certain of that. I need God to be greater. I settle my heart on the thought of that, and then I begin to consider again.

I would need God to be generous. For this problem to be resolved, things cannot stay the way they are. Both God and I know that is true. God would have to be generous with us; He would have to bless us in ways that are different from the way things are now.

And along those same lines, He would have to be abundant. This problem won't take care of itself in one afternoon, with one answer. It will require time. Not just once blessed, but blessed time and again. An abundance of blessings.

It is a lot to ask.

I consider it for a minute and decide it is too much to ask.

Not because He isn't already all of those things, and not because He isn't capable of all of those things. It just feels like it's too much to ask for Him to be all of those things for me, in my life, right now. Maybe I should ask for just one of those things.

In thinking this through, it dawns on me how I limit God. How maybe I place my own restrictions on Him. *Why do I place restrictions on Him?* The thought unsettles me. I don't do that when I am seeking help for other people. I am really good at asking God, at praying, at having faith *for other people.* The reality slams into me. Why do I limit God in my own life?

Even with the understanding of this, I still feel uncomfortable with the asking. For the first time in a long time,

I allow myself to become vulnerable again. My prayer comes from a place of weakness; I reach for the understanding of this. "Is it all right?" I ask from a heart made humble. "Is it all right for me to ask for these three things?"

I feel the peace of it, the same way I did in the hospital room, the same peace that filled my room on those late nights when Josh was three, the peace I discovered during the months and months of bed rest. I recognize the peace, so I pour my whole heart into the asking. "Please, God, will You be great, and generous, and abundant in my life?" The prayer ends there. I don't ask for the solutions I think I need. I don't go over the to-do list. I don't tell Him how I think it could be resolved.

I just ask Him to be great, generous, and abundant.

And my soul fills with the peace of it.

It's been a long time since I have felt peace like this. But the learning isn't over yet. Again, a prompting settles into my heart. *You need to remember this conversation.* I smile. I know the truth of this. I will return home, to my crazy life, to the endless demands and the relentless schedule, and I will forget. In two weeks I will forget that I even came to the beach.

I decide I will find a seashell to mark the conversation. When I return home I will set it in the window over my sink, and I will remember. I began walking where the water skims over the wet sand. It is low tide. Perfect for finding seashells. I scan the beach, taking in the colors of the shells lying in the sand: purple, white, gray, iridescent. They are beautiful. There is something in me that longs to find one worthy of this conversation, of this learning. It dawns on me exactly what type of shell would be perfect: a sand dollar. It is my favorite type of seashell. The conditions are right; so is the location. This isn't too much to ask. So I do. "Please, help me to find a sand dollar to remember this conversation."

I move out where the water is deeper. I know where the sand dollars wait. Just below the surf, hidden just below the sand. For ten minutes I walk and I search, until finally under the clear water I see the white curve sticking out from under the film of brown sand. I pick it up gently and cup it in my hands. It is perfect. White. The gray flower stenciled onto the raised backside is intricate in design. I will take it home, this gift from the sea, and set it in the window, and I will remember.

We still have two hours at the beach, so I continue walking, and as I walk I gather. Picking up the fragile white circles hidden under the brown silt until the crook of my arm is filled. Until it is time to go.

That night I spread out a towel and line up the sand dollars carefully. I want to take all of them home to show Greg. We have never brought this many sand dollars home from one trip to the beach. He will be impressed; I smile thinking how impressed he will be. It really is remarkable, how many there are. I lay them out, one by one, in lines across the turquoise terry cloth, and gently roll the towel over them. I want to protect them for the journey. It is when I am almost finished, just as I am laying the last of them out, that one final message whispers to my heart.

Remember, you asked for one.

The realization of it settles over me softly, sweetly, and I feel the sting of tears in my eyes. *I asked for one.* I unwrap the towel and begin to count. There are seventy-five sand dollars in all—an unexpected witness of God's greatness, and His generosity, and His abundance. There, on the beach, an answer had come. I had experienced the realness of God. My problem had not been resolved, but God had shown me that He could be generous and abundant in my life. Without question, He had shown it. I had experienced His greatness. God, Creator of the universe, infinite, had once again become intimate. I had experienced His goodness. He was giving me reason to trust. He didn't take away the problem, it wasn't resolved, it wasn't fixed, but He reminded me that He could.

He could be great. He could be generous. He could be abundant. He could be all of it for me. It is who He already is. All I had to do was ask.

What Do You Need God to Be?

It is amazing what changing a prayer will do for a life. Amazing how it creates new opportunity, how it opens up the potential for what God is capable of. But it requires stopping for a minute, moving away from the routine, looking at the asking in a way that hasn't been done before. And I wonder, *what do you need God to be right now?*

It is in the days that follow my experience on the beach that I really come to understand how my relationship with God is different when I allow Him to *be* instead of dictating what I want Him to *do*. And it's not just my relationship that is different. My prayers are different now. They have been ever since I returned from the beach. When I came home it wasn't just one sand dollar that I placed in the window; I carefully set all seventy-five in a square glass vase so that I could see the intricate detail of every single one. And when I look at them there, they become a gentle reminder: *ask what I can be for you, not just what I can do for you. Ask what I can be.* And I see how the asking is tethering me firmly to the reality of who He already is.

Good. Trustworthy. Faithful.

I am learning that who He is *is* what He provides. I must remember this. In this moment He is exactly what I need Him to be, and He has the capacity for what I need tomorrow.

Yes, this—this is the God I believe in.

I hold on to Him for a time, but then, as it does with all good things, the rawness begins to fade. I don't notice it right away. I should, but I don't. I see how winter melts away into spring, how the peonies bloom in all of their pale pink glory, how the days start to last longer. As the time moves forward I am aware of the waiting, how I am still waiting for the answers to come. And every day, every single day, from the day I return home from Mexico and the beach, I continue to pray. For God to be great, and abundant, and generous. I put my whole heart into that prayer, and I wait. Maybe God meant for that Mexico experience to be so memorable, for those sand dollars in the kitchen window to be just tangible enough that I wouldn't give up praying, because it isn't long before all of the details of my life suggest that maybe I should.

> In this moment He is exactly what I *need* Him to be, and He has the capacity for what I *need* tomorrow.

You remember those things on my to-do list *before* my prayer at the beach? The ones I had been praying about for forever? They didn't simply not happen, as if He hadn't heard me; instead, the exact *opposite* of what I had been asking for came to pass. My life began unraveling right before my eyes. The weight of it rested heavy on my heart. It brought back all the questions of my soul, *and maybe I didn't understand God after all.* Instead of seeing a change for the better, it seemed as if every venture in my life had taken a turn for the worse. God didn't just ignore the to-do list; He wiped the to-do list clean. He erased all of it. *Perhaps He wanted a fresh start.* I have to be honest with you: I panicked. I questioned Him just the way I always have. *Why? Why, God?* I felt the fear rush in, and in the rushing of it I felt the trust slipping out. In the last second I remembered, just before the trust was completely gone, how I was going to let God lead. How this time I was going to let God work out the miracle. How I was going to lean into His capacity, not mine. So I calmed my heart, and then I did what I had been telling myself I was going to do—I traced the goodness; I let go of the fear; I asked God to be great, abundant, and generous; and then I entered into the waiting place with a heart full of resolution.

The Waiting Place

I know this waiting place. I have been here before.

But this time I approach things differently. When it feels like time is moving slowly, when it feels like it isn't moving at all, I remind myself that just because time is standing still doesn't mean that God is. He is working here within the waiting. Orchestrating. Making necessary adjustments, prompting for course corrections. Through the intricate details of the miracle in the making, He is preparing to show me exactly what He can be.

I rest in the promise of that for a time, but it isn't long before I realize there is something else that will be required of me here in the waiting place, that God has something more to teach me. The learning comes through scripture—stories I have heard time and again. Yes, I have heard them, but there is one parallel I have never noticed until now. I lean into the truth of it: God knew where the Promised Land was all along, but Moses didn't. God knew what the finished ark would look like, but Noah didn't. God knew exactly how Egypt would be prepared for the famine, but Joseph didn't. Finding the Promised Land, building the ark, and preparing Egypt required more than simply praying for the miracle to take place and then waiting; each required a willingness to listen and then to act. I begin to realize that just praying for what I need God to be is not enough. There are things God will need from me.

The truth of it is that the waiting isn't a place for holding still, for remaining idle. It is a place for gaining strength, for learning to listen, for being led in the right direction, *His direction,* one small step at a time. And maybe the most important part of the waiting place is this learning how to listen, because I don't have any idea where to go next. Honestly, I don't even know what miracle this path is leading to. The answers come slowly, and I'm learning that God's first answer doesn't always let you see the end result. His way is to take things step by step. One small step at a time.

And what if every step is the miracle?

It is as I choose to take each small step down His path instead of mine that the answers begin to come. I realize with those first answers that there will be more to follow, that as God continues to answer I must continue to act. Through the process I can't help but wonder, *am I willing to pay the price that each new answer will cost?*

I feel the stretch of the growing that is taking place, the tethering as I lean into trust, the surety within each small step that this new direction is right, and I feel the truth of it settle into my soul.

Maybe the waiting place is where we really come to understand God.

The Next Right Step

When Saul breathed out threats and slaughter against the disciples of the Lord, had he asked God if this was the course he should take? Or was it his own strategy, his own design, the way he felt he should live out his beliefs? The letters he requested to take to Damascus, the ones that would allow him to bring the men and women bound to Jerusalem—had he asked God if that was His will? Or was it his own agenda and the agenda of conspiring minds that directed his path?

Was Saul busy living out his own to-do list for God?

I read in Acts chapter nine, and this time I don't focus on the events of the story—on Saul with the letters on the road to Damascus, or the conversation in the middle of that road that changed his perspective. Instead I focus on the waiting that begins the very moment Saul asks the question that will change the direction of his life.

"Lord, what wilt thou have me to do?" (Acts 9:6).

The answer doesn't come right away. Saul waits, blind for three days without seeing, until a certain disciple comes to him. Ananias. I search the meaning of this name and I smile.

Graciously given of the Lord. I can trace the goodness here, in this part of the story, and I know what will come immediately after tracing the goodness: a test of trust.

It is not hard to imagine this waiting place. Saul in darkness, stumbling, frightened. Requiring help to dress, to sit in a chair, to find his bed. Waiting for the knock to come at the door. I can't even begin to comprehend the amount of trust it required for Saul to let Ananias in. The condition God had placed Saul in left him incapable of defending himself. Ananias, the Christian standing outside the door, had every right to hold animosity against Saul, hatred even. Surely Saul expected to find a man whose heart was filled with judgment, anger, and resentment. But Ananias honored God's appointment, and Saul let him in, and I love that the first name Ananias calls Saul, of all the names he could have called him, is *brother.* "Brother Saul, the Lord . . . hath sent me" (Acts 9:17). In that moment, in the very moment when trust is built, the blindness falls from Saul's eyes, and he can see.

I recognize the pattern. First, I trace God's goodness in Ananias. Then, I read how Saul lets go of what holds him back, his blindness, how he learns to trust. Last, I read how Saul leans into God's capacity.

I go back to the question Saul asked God—*what would you have me do?*—and immediately the truth of it strikes my heart. Instead of giving God a to-do list, Saul asks for one. And then he waits. It is over a decade before Paul begins his ministry, before he fully discovers exactly what God has in mind for him to do. *Over a decade in the waiting place.* I watch Paul in this. He asks. He waits. I think about the waiting and I realize the answers probably did not come all at once—that while he was being strengthened, perhaps he was also being led. Paul set off on the road to Damascus; he took the first step, and then the next right step, and the next right step, until years later he was exactly where he needed to be, just when God needed him to be there.

> He was *exactly* where he needed to be, just when God *needed* him to be there.

And I wonder, *where am I on my own road to Damascus? And when was the last time I asked God what He needed me to do?*

It is February, and I travel halfway across the country to meet with a woman who is not afraid to reach across religious boundaries in order to further God's work. For two days I sit at her feet and I am taught. I take pages and pages of notes; I don't want to miss a word of her wisdom, of her insight, of her expertise. When the time is up, I gather my belongings and prepare to go. "It is impossible, what I am trying to do—I want you to know I understand that," I tell her as I prepare to leave. *I wouldn't even be here, wouldn't have taken your time, if I didn't feel that God had led me to come.* She nods her head; she knows this. She has heard the story, my story, before. We both know the truth of it—that she is the one who honored God's prompting; she is the one who allowed me to come. She is my Ananias.

I turn back before I leave and ask the question that is hanging on my heart. "If you could give me one word of advice before I leave, knowing all of this, knowing everything, what would it be?" The question is sincere, and I prepare myself for the answer. Because I know she will be honest. Her gift is her ability to be genuine. Even with this. I watch her consider for a minute. She understands what I am up against, the way it has never worked out before, the reality that it probably won't this time. I know her answer won't paint a pretty picture, that she won't set out for me an unreal expectation. It is not her way.

In the waiting for the answer I hold on to the learning from this journey. I trace the goodness, and I believe. I let go of the doubt, and I trust. I rest in the promise of what I have asked God to be, the assurance of who He already is. When she finally responds, her kind eyes and her sincere answer fill me with hope, and I know the advice is exactly what I need to hear.

"Just take the next right step."

THE REFLECTING PLACE

It is summertime, and I am eleven. In the afternoons, when my mother lets me, I walk to the creek down the street from our blue Tudor home. The water runs slowly, just over my ankles. It is cool from the shade of the century-old trees that line the banks. A thick rope hangs over the middle of the creek, suspended from one of the branches of the largest tree. I take hold of the knot at the bottom and walk over to the bank on the grassy side. When I am ready, I grab the upper knot with both hands and jump, lifting my feet and setting them safely on the lower knot. I rest my weight against the rope, against the sureness of the strands of jute woven together for strength, and I swing. I close my eyes and get lost in the sound of the water moving over the river rock, the leaves rustling in the trees, and I lean into the rhythm of the rope moving back and forth, back and forth, and back and forth again.

I am decades older now, but there is still something about a constant rhythm that soothes my soul. The crashing of waves, the drum that beats out the pace of a song, the rocking back and forth of a hammock. I lean into the sureness of the rhythm, and my soul finds peace there. It is why I love this moment of reflection at the end of every day; the soothing that comes before the slumber. It has become the rhythm of my life. I find myself leaning into it, letting it soothe my soul.

Perhaps you find yourself looking forward to it also. Tonight I will add one last piece.

I focus on what I need God to be.

I ponder the needs in my life, the wanting, the aching, the resolutions that are beyond my own capacity, and I lean into His. I have started a different list. Instead of a to-do list, it is a list of what I need God to be based on who He already is. Every time I turn to His Word, I look for the witnesses of His capacity, of who He is. The Healer, the Deliverer, Sure, Merciful, Powerful, my Refuge, Protection. When I find each new description, I write it down. I am keeping a journal. A list of His characteristics that I do not want to forget.

Perhaps you will start a journal like this. In case you feel inclined to, I have included the beginning of one in the appendix of this book. It includes all of the words I have gathered in the journal that I currently keep at my bedside. As I pray, I go over this new list and I ask God for what I need Him to be in my life right now.

There is peace in the asking. Encouraging, restoring, settling peace. I lean into the peace and then I prepare myself to listen, because this last piece, this necessary pause, will require listening.

Once I have asked for what I need God to be, I ask Him what He would have me do.

And then, I wait. For the whisper I know will come. The prompting. The flash of insight. The next right step.

Yes, every night it is the same.

First, I trace God's goodness. I express my thanks, and I

am reminded how gratitude reveals God's generosity. Next, I try to recognize what is blinding me, what is holding me back. I let it go, and I learn what it is to trust. Then, I go over the list of words in my journal to remind me of God's character, and I humbly petition God for what I need Him to be. Last, I ask the question that I know will change the outcome of my life one small step at a time. "Lord, what would you have me do?"

It is life-changing, what I have discovered through the process.

The tracing the goodness and expressing of gratitude.

The letting go, which leads to trust.

The leaning into God's capacity for what I need Him to be.

The asking for what He would have me do.

Every night it is the same, this rhythm that has become my way of life. I trace the goodness. I trust. I lean in. I ask. I trace, I trust, I lean in, I ask, I trace. . . .

Again, and again, and again, I lean into the rhythm and I find peace there. The process is changing me. It is redefining the course of my life.

Lean into God's Capacity

The Understanding

What was the beginning of spring with its pale pink peonies turns into July with its burst of fireworks, late summer nights, and fresh watermelon. Fall settles in next, the red fiery oaks and golden yellow aspen brilliant against the mountain backdrop. And then the snowflakes fall. It is there, within the transitions, that I begin to notice it—softly in the beginning, like the winter flakes that glide gently to the dark earth. The first ones barely leave a mark, but as they continue to swirl in greater number, slowly they begin to gather. I see the whiteness and realize it is made up of individual flakes, each intricate in design, sent from heaven to blanket my world.

I sit on the warm hearth next to the blazing fire and pause to consider the individual, intricate, heaven-sent blessings that surround me daily. As I gather them together, understanding comes. Looking back, I realize how after the first doors had slammed closed, the windows of heaven had opened, and I see that the blessings had begun to fall like a whisper. The blessings are so good, so exactly what I need, and yet so opposite of what I had been asking for that I might have missed them if I hadn't been watching. They come in ways that are unexpected, with timing I hadn't foreseen. The understanding settles in slowly like a winter sunrise after the storm, spreading light softly into my soul.

And maybe God's will is too good for us to know. Beyond our imagination. Exceeding our expectation.

I look out over the whiteness at the boughs of the pine trees that have been heaped upon with flakes of delicate beauty, each His intricate design, and I begin to realize what I wish I had known all along. Perhaps God has something entirely different in mind for me than what I had ever anticipated.

Something better.

> Perhaps God has something entirely *different* in mind for me than what I had ever anticipated. **Something better.**

He Forgets Not His Own

Life is designed to make us question. It is full of a series of events meant to define a soul. And those two questions that we all ask when life becomes uncertain—*Is God good? Can He be trusted?*—what if they aren't meant to push us away from God? What if they are divinely designed to lead us closer to Him?

I ask those questions now and I no longer wait for life to show me the answer; I ask God to. His response is unexpected and yet it is the same every time: *If you want to know if I am good, if I can be trusted, come and see.*

This God who met Moses next to a burning bush, and Joseph in the prison, and Saul on the road to Damascus, the one from the University of Utah hospital room, the dark nights of raising a three-year-old with diabetes, and the recovery room after the surgery to save Grace—He wants a personal relationship. He meets us in the vulnerable places, in the raw moments. He beckons to us in the most intimate spaces of our life with an invitation that isn't new. It's the same one Jesus extended to the Apostles, the one that leads to the beginning of a life devoted to Him.

Come and see.

If I want to know His goodness, I will have to come and see, to discover it for myself. That's how I will learn to recognize Him when the sun shines over wildflower fields; to feel for Him when the storms roll over the unsheltered places in my soul. It is an ongoing choice, this choosing God. Yes, it is true. With each new struggle, with each fresh painful encounter, I will find myself questioning. I can't help but question. *Why? Why, God?* Daily I will be given the opportunity to choose. Where will I turn when the sky comes crashing down? Where will I reach when I am in the depths of despair? What will I hold on to when the ground slips from beneath my feet? When my answer to those questions is *God*, that's when life becomes miraculous. Those personal encounters will lead me to glimpse His glory.

I am learning that He will meet me in the unexpected places, bringing His goodness, giving me cause to trust, reminding me of His capacity. And maybe when I question, it is simply a sign that my soul is longing to understand Him better. I must remember the truth of that.

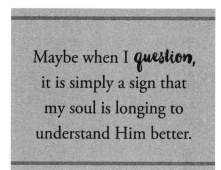

Maybe when I *question*, it is simply a sign that my soul is longing to understand Him better.

This journey to know God is becoming the journey of my life. I want it to consume my every moment; I want it to become my rhythm, my walk, my daily routine.

Maybe you long for this also.

We could walk this journey together, you and I.

Let's make a promise to each other right now that every time our soul begins to question—*Is God good? Can He be trusted?*—we won't shut our hearts to the reality of God. No. Let's promise that those questions will always be viewed as an invitation to enter in. To come and see.

To discover the reality of God in an ordinary life.

Where we are right now, this moment, this part of the journey, God already knows about it. And tomorrow? He will be there. Surrounding us with goodness. Giving us reason to trust. Defining His capacity. The way He always has. The way He always will. It is the daily rediscovery of that truth that has the potential to become the greatest journey of a life. Of this, I am certain.

Yes, dear friend, God is good.

He always has been, and He always will be.

And He can be trusted with anything your heart holds.

Anything.

Even this.

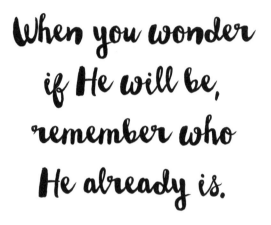

*When you wonder
if He will be,
remember who
He already is.*

This is just the **BEGINNING**. A study guide.
A resource. A list for you to add to, take notes
on, and use as a guide in making your own.

Able

ROMANS 4:21

Being fully persuaded that, what he had promised, he was able also to perform.

2 CORINTHIANS 9:8

And God is able to make all grace abound toward you; that ye, always having all sufficiency in all things, may abound to every good work.

_____

_____

_____

_____

_____

_____

_____

_____

Among Us

JOSHUA 22:31

This day we perceive that the Lord is among us.

JOSHUA 3:5

And Joshua said unto the people, Sanctify yourselves: for to morrow the Lord will do wonders among you.

_____

_____

_____

_____

_____

_____

The Beginning of Wisdom

PSALM 111:10

The fear of the Lord is the beginning of wisdom: a good understanding have all they that do his commandments: his praise endureth for ever.

Counselor

ISAIAH 9:6

For unto us a child is born, unto us a son is given: and the government shall be upon his shoulder: and his name shall be called Wonderful, Counsellor, The mighty God, The everlasting Father, The Prince of Peace.

Discerner of the Heart

HEBREWS 4:12

For the word of God is quick, and powerful, and sharper than any two-edged sword, piercing even to the dividing asunder of soul and spirit, and of the joints and marrow, and is a discerner of the thoughts and intents of the heart.

Faithful

2 THESSALONIANS 3:3

But the Lord is faithful, who shall stablish you, and keep you from evil.

1 CORINTHIANS 10:13

There hath no temptation taken you but such as is common to man: but God is faithful, who will not suffer you to be tempted above that ye are able; but will with the temptation also make a way to escape, that ye may be able to bear it.

Forgiving

PSALM 103:2-3

Bless the Lord, O my soul, and forget not all his benefits: Who forgiveth all thine iniquities.

_____

_____

_____

_____

_____

_____

_____

_____

_____

Full of Compassion

PSALM 111:4

He hath made his wonderful works to be remembered: the Lord is . . . full of compassion.

_____

_____

_____

_____

_____

_____

_____

_____

_____

Generous

PSALM 86:5

For thou, Lord, art good, and ready to forgive; and plenteous in mercy unto all them that call upon thee.

ISAIAH 30:23

Then shall he give the rain of thy seed, that thou shalt sow the ground withal; and bread of the increase of the earth, and it shall be fat and plenteous: in that day shall thy cattle feed in large pastures.

_____

_____

_____

_____

_____

_____

_____

_____

Good

PSALM 34:8

O taste and see that the Lord is good: blessed is the man that trusteth in him.

_____

_____

_____

_____

_____

_____

_____

Gracious

PSALM 111:4

He hath made his wonderful works to be remembered: the Lord is gracious.

Greater

EXODUS 18:11

Now I know that the Lord is greater than all gods: for in the thing wherein they dealt proudly he was above them.

PSALM 95:3

For the Lord is a great God, and a great King above all gods.

JOB 33:12

Behold, in this thou art not just: I will answer thee, that God is greater than man.

He That Fights for You

JOSHUA 23:3

And ye have seen all that the Lord your God hath done unto all these nations because of you; for the Lord your God is he that hath fought for you.

_____

_____

_____

_____

_____

_____

_____

He Which Goeth before Thee

DEUTERONOMY 9:3

Understand therefore this day, that the Lord thy God is he which goeth over before thee; as a consuming fire he shall destroy them, and he shall bring them down before thy face: so shalt thou drive them out, and destroy them quickly, as the Lord hath said unto thee.

_____

_____

_____

_____

_____

_____

_____

Healer

PSALM 103:2-3

Bless the Lord, O my soul, and forget not all his benefits: . . . who healeth all thy diseases.

_____

_____

_____

_____

_____

_____

_____

Hope

JEREMIAH 17:7

Blessed is the man that trusteth in the Lord, and whose hope the Lord is.

PSALM 39:7

And now, Lord, what wait I for? my hope is in thee.

PSALM 71:5

For thou art my hope, O Lord God: thou art my trust from my youth.

_____

_____

_____

_____

_____

_____

_____

In All Things

DEUTERONOMY 4:7

For what nation is there so great, who hath God so nigh unto them, as the Lord our God is in all things that we call upon him for?

In This Place

GENESIS 28:16

And Jacob awaked out of his sleep, and he said, Surely the Lord is in this place; and I knew it not.

Liberty

2 CORINTHIANS 3:17

Now the Lord is that Spirit: and where the Spirit of the Lord is, there is liberty.

_____

_____

_____

_____

_____

_____

_____

_____

_____

Light

1 JOHN 1:5

This then is the message which we have heard of him, and declare unto you, that God is light, and in him is no darkness at all.

_____

_____

_____

_____

_____

_____

_____

_____

_____

_____

Love

1 JOHN 4:8

He that loveth not knoweth not God; for God is love.

_____
_____
_____
_____
_____
_____
_____
_____

Merciful

PSALM 103:8

The Lord is merciful and gracious, slow to anger, and plenteous in mercy.

_____
_____
_____
_____
_____
_____
_____
_____
_____

Mighty
JOB 36:5
Behold, God is mighty, and despiseth not any: he is mighty in strength and wisdom.

My Defense
PSALM 59:9
Because of his strength will I wait upon thee: for God is my defence.

My Deliverer

PSALM 18:2

The Lord is . . . my deliverer; my God, my strength, in whom I will trust.

My Fortress

PSALM 18:2

The Lord is . . . my fortress . . . in whom I will trust.

My Helper

HEBREWS 13:6

So that we may boldly say, The Lord is my helper, and I will not fear what man shall do unto me.

PSALM 54:4

Behold, God is mine helper: the Lord is with them that uphold my soul.

_____

_____

_____

_____

_____

_____

_____

My Light

PSALM 27:1

The Lord is my light and my salvation; whom shall I fear?

_____

_____

_____

_____

_____

_____

_____

_____

My Portion

PSALM 16:5

The Lord is the portion of mine inheritance and of my cup: thou maintainest my lot.

LAMENTATIONS 3:24

The Lord is my portion, saith my soul; therefore will I hope in him.

_____

_____

_____

_____

_____

_____

_____

My Rock

PSALM 18:2

The Lord is my rock.

_____

_____

_____

_____

_____

_____

_____

_____

_____

My Shepherd
PSALM 23:1-3

The Lord is my shepherd; I shall not want. He maketh me to lie down in green pastures: he leadeth me beside the still waters. He restoreth my soul: he leadeth me in the paths of righteousness for his name's sake.

_____

_____

_____

_____

_____

_____

_____

My Stronghold
NAHUM 1:7

The Lord is good, a strong hold in the day of trouble; and he knoweth them that trust in him.

_____

_____

_____

_____

_____

_____

_____

_____

On My Side

PSALM 118:6

The Lord is on my side; I will not fear: what can man do unto me?

Our Defense

PSALM 89:18

For the Lord is our defence; and the Holy One of Israel is our king.

Perfect

PSALM 19:7

The law of the Lord is perfect, converting the soul.

Powerful

PSALM 29:4

The voice of the Lord is powerful; the voice of the Lord is full of majesty.

ISAIAH 40:29

He giveth power to the faint; and to them that have no might he increaseth strength.

Protection

PSALM 18:2

The Lord is . . . my strength, in whom I will trust; my buckler, and the horn of my salvation, and my high tower.

Redeeming

PSALM 103:2, 4

Bless the Lord, O my soul, and forget not all his benefits: . . . Who redeemeth thy life from destruction; who crowneth thee with lovingkindness and tender mercies.

Refuge

DEUTERONOMY 33:27

The eternal God is thy refuge, and underneath are the everlasting arms: and he shall thrust out the enemy from before thee; and shall say, Destroy them.

Strength

EXODUS 15:2

The Lord is my strength and song, and he is become my salvation: he is my God, and I will prepare him an habitation; my father's God, and I will exalt him.

NEHEMIAH 8:10

Then he said unto them, Go your way, eat the fat, and drink the sweet, and send portions unto them for whom nothing is prepared: for this day is holy unto our Lord: neither be ye sorry; for the joy of the Lord is your strength.

2 SAMUEL 22:33

God is my strength and power: and he maketh my way perfect.

Sure

PSALM 19:7

The testimony of the Lord is sure, making wise the simple.

_____

_____

_____

_____

_____

_____

_____

_____

Tender

LUKE 1:78

Through the tender mercy of our God; whereby the dayspring from on high hath visited us.

_____

_____

_____

_____

_____

_____

_____

_____

_____

There

EZEKIEL 48:35

And the name of the city from that day shall be, The Lord is there.

_____

_____

_____

_____

_____

_____

_____

_____

_____

Thy Keeper

PSALM 121:5

The Lord is thy keeper: the Lord is thy shade upon thy right hand.

_____

_____

_____

_____

_____

_____

_____

_____

_____

True

JOHN 3:33

He that hath received his testimony hath set to his seal that God is true.

Upon All Them for Good That Seek Him

EZRA 8:22

The hand of our God is upon all them for good that seek him.

With Us

NUMBERS 14:9

Only rebel not ye against the Lord, neither fear ye the people of the land; for they are bread for us: their defence is departed from them, and the Lord is with us: fear them not.

JOSHUA 1:9

Have not I commanded thee? Be strong and of a good courage; be not afraid, neither be thou dismayed: for the Lord thy God is with thee whithersoever thou goest.

_____

_____

_____

_____

_____

_____

_____

_____

Wondrous

PSALM 86:10

For thou art great, and doest wondrous things: thou art God alone.

_____

_____

_____

_____

_____

_____

_____

Your Way Wherein You Go

JUDGES 18:6

And the priest said unto them, Go in peace: before the Lord is your way wherein ye go.

_____

_____

_____

_____

_____

_____

_____

_____

_____

_____

_____

_____

_____

"But now thus saith the
Lord that created thee, . . .
Fear not: for I have redeemed thee,
I have called thee by thy name;
thou art **mine**.
When thou passest through the waters,
I will be **with** thee;
and through the rivers,
they shall not **overflow** thee:
when thou walkest through the fire,
thou shalt not be **burned**;
neither shall the flame kindle upon thee.
For I am the Lord thy God,
the Holy One of Israel,
thy Saviour: . . .
Since thou wast **precious** in my sight, . . .
I have loved thee. . . .
Fear not:
for I am **with** thee."

ISAIAH 43:1-5

THE JOURNAL

THE JOURNAL

THE JOURNAL

THE JOURNAL

THE JOURNAL

THE JOURNAL

Acknowledgments

At the end one can't help but reflect back to those who have been there since the beginning. Where are the words that capture the overflowing of a grateful heart?

Laurel Day and Chris Schoebinger for not only allowing me to walk a different road but accompanying me on the journey; Lysa Terkeurst for your mentoring heart and guiding thoughts; Chrislyn Woolston for your tireless belief and constant encouragement along the way; David Butler for stretching me to discover the message that wanted to be shared; Sarah Smith, who walked the Mexico beach with me those many months ago; and Nish Weiseth, who believed all along that the story of the sand dollar was one worth telling.

For the Ensign Peak team, Heidi Taylor, Lisa Mangum, Tracy Keck, Heather Ward, Richard Erickson, and Rachael Ward, who work tirelessly behind the scenes to bring ideas to life, taking thoughts in a heart and creating words on pages, bound together, and offered up.

For those who have heard this story on an airplane, in a hospital room, or from an audience and connected through a kind word, email, or letter, for reminding me that learning to trust sometimes requires leaning on each other. How one who has walked the path before can accompany another on the journey. How God sends us to each other. I love how He is good like that.

Tamu Smith, Zandra Vranes, Whitney Permann, Stephanie and Heath Taylor, Tasha Murphy, Hilary Weeks, Chase Murphy, Meg and J.J. Tenney, Steve and Heather Beers, Macy Robison, and McKinley Oswald, dedicated friends who read these words and added some of their own. I treasure your wisdom.

Caleb, Maria, Garett, Natalie, Kingston, Josh, Janaye, Megan, J.J., and Grace, there is no one I would rather do life with. My heart overflows with love for each of you. We are so blessed.

Greg, who gives me strength, stills the rhythm of my life, and stands beside. You are and always will be the love of my life.

To all these . . .

Thank you.